The Last Jews of Rădăuţi

The Last

Text by Ayşe Gürsan-Salzmann

Jews of Rădăuţi

Photographs by Laurence Salzmann

THE DIAL PRESS

DOUBLEDAY & COMPANY, INC.
GARDEN CITY, NEW YORK 1983

Published by
The Dial Press

Manufactured in the United States of America

First printing

Book design executed by Giorgetta Bell McRee

Library of Congress Cataloging in Publication Data

Gürsan-Salzman, Ayşe.
The last Jews of Rădăuţi.

1. Jews—Romania—Rădăuţi—Social life and customs.
2. Holocaust survivors—Romania—Rădăuţi. 3. Rădăuţi
(Romania)—Ethnic relations. 4. Rădăuţi (Romania)—
Description—Views. 5. Gürsan-Salzmann, Ayşe.
6. Salzmann, Laurence. I. Salzmann, Laurence. II. Title.
DS135.R72R334   1983   949.8′1   82–22176
ISBN 0–385–27808–X

This book is dedicated to the memory of two men who opened their homes and hearts to us while we lived in their community. They are Josef Tirnauer, the rabbi, and Abraham Kern, the shoemaker.

To these friends we owe a special tribute.

Contents

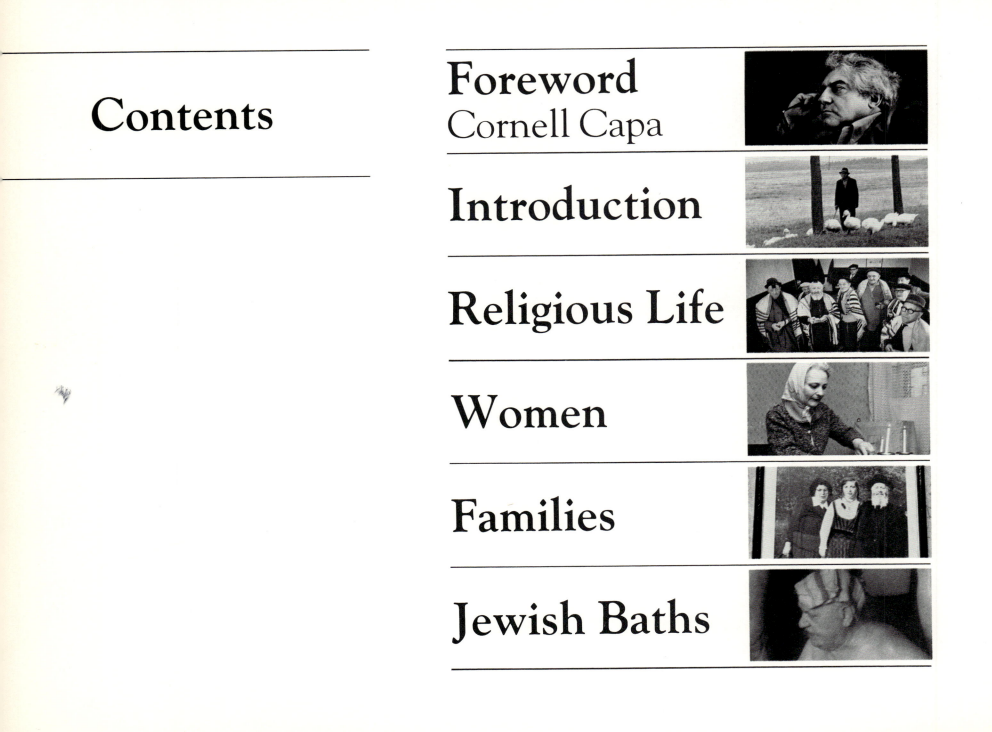

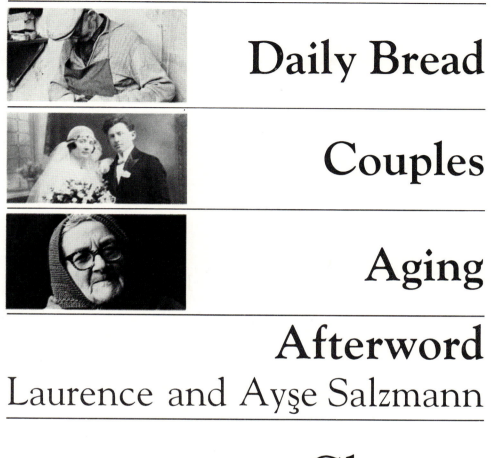

Foreword

Cornell Capa

The Salzmanns' book on the Jews of Rădăuţi is a modern miracle. The miracle is manifold: how a handful of people managed to survive the Holocaust and straggle back to their homes in Rădăuţi; how two young people, the Salzmanns, dedicated their hearts, brains, and skill to fix and transmit that experience for us; and how everybody involved, governments, foundations, and the people themselves, opened their doors so that now we can hold this special jewel of vanishing life in our hands.

The content of this book is an affirmation that nothing can be more interesting, gripping, and illuminating than the fabric of real life. The humor and drama infinite in its human variety evokes wonderment and recognition. Simple words and images woven with poetic sincerity captivate and touch hearts in a way that no artifice could equal. It is a passion play in a simple setting with real people as actors reliving the nightmares of the past, play-acting the present, and giving unmistakable hints of an ominous future.

The life stories of Rabbi Tirnauer, Fräulein Grünglas, and the Dankners are especially gripping. The perspective of four decades of life, arrested for a fleeting moment of two years by the Salzmanns, gives substance of this microcosm of Eastern European Jewish life.

The Salzmanns instinctively understood the strength of their story and the necessary modesty of their own contribution to it. Because of this understanding, their roles as photographer and writer preserved the heart of the fragment of life that is Rădăuţi.

CORNELL CAPA
January 1982

Laurence's initiation to the Jewish community in Rădăuţi took place when he was asked to be the tenth man for an early morning minyan at the Main Temple. The men present are, from left to right, Srul Beer (furrier), Kriegsman (barber), Rabbi Tirnauer, Moses Lehrer (glazier), Ginzer (security officer), Herman Gelber (chauffeur), Mendel Sontag (tailor), Schonblum and Meir Sontag (Jewish Committee functionaries).

Introduction

In the fall of 1974 my husband, Laurence Salzmann, went to Romania on a Fulbright grant in photography. He was interested in working in an Eastern European country that had a strong folk tradition. He also had vivid memories of an aunt who used to reminisce fondly about the Romania she'd known as a young girl.

When he arrived in Bucharest, he decided to collaborate on a project with folklorists from the National Folklore Institute. There, friends suggested that Laurence visit Rădăuţi (pronounced RA-da-oo-ts) to see the colorful peasant market and the famous painted Moldavian monasteries nearby, built by Stephen the Great. Little did they or he know that he would be living in Rădăuţi for the next two years.

One of his first trips was to Maramures, a region known for its distinctive folk culture. While there, Laurence visited Elie Wiesel's birthplace, the small town of Sighet. He had seen *Sighet-Sighet*, Wiesel's film about the writer's return there after the war, and had been profoundly moved by it. Laurence found the same empty streets in the Jewish quarter that had been shown in the film. A solemn white cement monument in memory of the Jews who had died at Auschwitz bore the following inscription:

> *In the month of May, in 1944, 38,000 Jewish citizens of the district*
> *of Maramures were exterminated in Nazi concentration camps. (Sur-*

*vivors were, later, liberated by the glorious Soviet Army.) We erect this monument in remembrance of the mass sufferings caused by Hitler's fascistic regime, and we continue to fight against Hitleristic imperialism so that such a crime against humanity does not ever occur again. ***

Continuing farther on his exploratory trip in the area, Laurence went on to the town of Rădăuţi. Up until 1918, Rădăuţi had been a part of the Austro-Hungarian Empire, and many of the older townspeople had attended German schools. Laurence was delighted to find that the Jews of Rădăuţi all spoke German, a language he had learned in college; he had no difficulty in understanding or being understood by them. They were willing to accept him as one of their own, and he felt culturally related to them.

By now his focus had become defined. He wanted his project to serve as an intimate, clear record of what small-town Jewish life was like today in an Eastern setting. He hoped that by concentrating on one community he would be able to make a statement about similar communities in other Eastern European countries such as Hungary and Poland.

He returned to the town in December 1974 and, having obtained the necessary permits from Bucharest, established his headquarters in the Hotel Rădăuţi.

According to the prominent Romanian historian Nicholas Iorga, Rădăuţi was first settled in prehistoric times. The name Rădăuţi came from a certain Rădu and his descendants. The suffix *ăuţi (esti)* means "his place" or "place of Radu" (Radu + uţi).

Friday market in Rădăuţi—a view from a distance. Peasants from villages as far as twenty kilometers from Rădăuţi visited the market, where vegetables, dairy products, flowers, pottery, clothing, fabrics, and live chickens were laid out on the wooden stalls.

---

* Translated from the Romanian.

In the fourteenth century Rădăuţi was something of a small market town and a trading center. One of the Moldavian princes made the town his capital. It did not remain as a capital for long, but it has continued as a market center right up to the present day.

The origins of the Jewish community of Rădăuţi are, to some extent, typical of several other small Romanian towns with Jewish populations: Dorohoi, Falticeni, Vatra Dornei, Botoshani, Siret, and Cimpulung-Moldovenesc (see map, page 139).

The Jews of Rădăuţi are descendants of those who came from Galicia, now part of Poland, during the mid-nineteenth century. The Bukovina region, or Buchenland (land of the beech trees), where Rădăuţi is located (see map, page 138), came under Austrian domination in 1774. Beginning in the late eighteenth century Jews traveled freely to the Bukovina region. The first arrivals in Rădăuţi were traders selling manufactured goods, such as textiles from Galicia, in return for which they bought local products, such as furs, wool, foodstuffs, and flax. Rădăuţi was favorably located on a major trade route running northwest–southeast through Poland, the Russian steppes, and the eastern Carpathians, following the Siret and Danube rivers into the seaports of the Black Sea.

A major part of this trade was carried on by the Jewish merchants. Today the sons and grandsons of these people are involved in similar pursuits, only acting as middlemen. They also continue the tradition of other small trades and crafts: miller, tailor, shoemaker, furrier. The Jews who came in the nineteenth century established inns in cities such as Suceava, Vatra Dornei, Siret, and Cernauti (see map, page 138.) Gradually Jewish communities evolved there.

As early as 1807 three Jewish families were listed as paying taxes in Rădăuţi. The first synagogue was built around 1830, followed by the cemetery. Prior to that the dead were buried in Siret. A Jewish ritual bath was established. In 1861 Bukovina became one of the seventeen Länder (provinces) of the Austrian Empire. Soon thereafter the emperor Franz Josef visited Rădăuţi; he was met by a group of the town's Jewish people, who petitioned him for land where they could erect a large synagogue. Franz Josef gave them a centrally located site near the marketplace and also provided some of the building materials. This synagogue, the main temple of Rădăuţi, is still standing.

The Jews occupied a special position within the Austrian Empire. In the Bukovina region, together with the ethnic Germans, they were fervent supporters of German culture. By the 1880s the Jewish population of Bukovina had reached 100,000 and the Jewish community of Rădăuţi numbered 3,452 within the total population of 11,162. During World War I Romania was an ally of the *entente* powers and in the Versailles peace settlement of 1917 was awarded Bukovina and Bessarabia (see map, page 138).

The Jews continued to play an important role in the business and cultural life of Rădăuţi. For a time, during the 1930s, the famous lieder singer Josef Schmidt was the cantor in the main synagogue. Life seemed safe and secure; few would have believed that in just a short time lives would be changed so drastically.

From 1938 to 1940 Romania came increasingly under German power. Germany needed Romania for its oil, grains, and meat. At the beginning of World War II Romania was allied with Poland. In July 1940 Romania lost Bessarabia and Bukovina to the Soviet Union. Hoping to recover these losses, Romania became Germany's most ardent satellite. The fascist Iron Guard became part of the government forces and instituted several pogroms in the cities of Iasi and Bucharest; however, it was in the provinces of Bukovina and Bessarabia, which Romania recaptured from the Soviet Union, that the Jewish population suffered the brunt of the Romanian destructive frenzy. According to the Tighiana agreement signed by German and Romanian military staffs in August 1941, a region in the Ukraine

between the Bug and Dniester rivers known as Transnistria (see map, page 141) was selected as the temporary dumping ground for Jews from Bessarabia and Bukovina. The Romanians, with certain qualifications, were to administer the camps in Transnistria, where Jews would be assigned to forced labor until military operations were concluded.

In September 1941 the Jews of Rădăuți were deported to Transnistria. Many died before even reaching the camps at Djurin, Kopaigorod, Mogilev, Tulchin, and elsewhere (see map, page 141). Forced labor, disease, hunger, and the ruthlessness of the captors further depleted the Jewish population. The ultimate goal of the Germans and the Romanian fascist government was to kill off all the Bukovinian Jews. What prevented this from taking place was the defeat of the German and Romanian forces at Stalingrad in early 1943. As the tides of war changed, so did the official Romanian policy toward the Jews who were still alive in Transnistria. Repatriation of the Jews of Bukovina began in early 1944. Those who returned to Bukovina were in poor health. Their homes had been destroyed and all their belongings had been taken away. Only one fourth of the pre–World War II Jewish population of Rădăuți (2,000 of the total population of 8,000) returned.

Eventually, help came from abroad, from JOINT (the International Jewish Organization), and from relatives of the townspeople living in the United States. In 1948 there was a large *aliya* to Israel. At this time the Romanian government nationalized all businesses and factories. This affected many of the town's Jews, who had only recently begun to rebuild their businesses. In the early 1950s a hundred Jews were sent to forced

---

Strada Putnei, known as *die Yiddengasse*, where many Jewish-owned shops used to be located. Since this photo was taken, the cobblestones have been replaced by an asphalt-topped road.

Roza Blum had a relatively spacious kitchen, with a modern gas range and oven. She invited me to use it when I needed to cook a meal. She seemed to enjoy watching me prepare my Turkish dishes, and tasting them.

labor camps for terms of up to five years for violating a law against possessing gold or foreign currency. In the 1960s and 1970s the government policy became more lenient on granting visas to Jews, so more left for Israel, West Germany, and the United States. In the last thirty years over 300,000 Romanian Jews have emigrated to Israel. Romania is the only Eastern Bloc country that maintains amicable and cooperative relations with Israel. In 1975 Romania was granted most-favored-nation status by the United States in anticipation of freer emigration laws. In July 1979 the leaders of thirty-three Jewish organizations in the United States recommended that the United States continue granting most-favored-nation status to Romania after reviewing the emigration policy for Jews.

I joined Laurence in Rădăuți during the spring of 1975. Together we began to devise methods of studying the community: collecting life histories and unraveling the underlying social structure, the network of social relationships within and between families. Some especially generous and well-informed people became our chief consultants, and we were able to visit many people in their homes. While I was collecting their histories, Laurence was taking photographs to illustrate them. As a woman I could sometimes communicate in ways that Laurence could not, but sometimes Laurence became *my* consultant: the religious life of the community was very important, but I, as a woman, could not participate in most of the rituals. All in all, we talked with more people than either of us could have reached working alone, and we had no difficulty coordinating their words with the images.

We were known in Rădăuți as *der Herr Laurenz* and *die Frau Ayşe*. When they saw us together, people greeted Laurence with a warm handshake and me with the chivalrous tradition of hand-kissing. Otherwise they would say to Laurence, "Where is your wife, when is she coming back?" or to me, "I haven't seen Laurence today, is he in town or in Bucharest?"

People saw us as a couple. Since we were invited or expected to be seen together, we felt comfortable about interacting with the people *not* in the roles of anthropologist and photographer, but as two people residing among them, interested in their families, stories, and cultural traditions.

Gradually we became part of their everyday experience. Some people we would visit only if formally invited. Others, such as Roza Blum and Margit Kamiel, encouraged us to visit them anytime, and even make use of their cooking facilities if we wished. Our relationships with the Kerns and the Tirnauer family were very special. There was an informal friendliness that surpassed ceremonious behavior. We respected their reticence about answering some of our questions, especially political and financial ones, and their wishes about not being photographed. We would occasionally stop at the Lehrers' framing shop during work hours. Mr. Lehrer and his wife always welcomed us even though they continued to do their work as we chatted. Then we would see our friends at the long lines outside the grocery stores (*alimentara*). They would be in pursuit of the same food staples—bread, sugar, oil, and cheese—as we were. Once I remember Mrs. Dankner asking me graciously if I would buy a package of butter for her family. Mr. Dankner had already bought one, and the manager would not give another one to Mrs. Dankner since he knew they were man and wife, and butter was a dear item. My question was, how could *I* get two if they wouldn't give two to her? Well, I was a *straiin* (foreigner), and people respected the wishes of a foreigner. She was right. I got two packages of butter without an argument.

We lived in a hotel room for twenty months (except for occasional visits to other regions of Romania), where we worked, cooked on a camping stove, and slept. The bay window in the west corner of our hotel room overlooked the main plaza of the town. By six o'clock every morning the pulse of life had begun. The footsteps of the workers and the peasants coming from nearby villages, the whistle of the train, the bread trucks

Mr. Malik and Laurence in the garden of Malik's home—one of those rare occasions when someone offered to take Laurence's picture.

xxiii

lining up in front of the grocery stores, all became familiar sounds to our ears. Toward noon each day the Jewish ritual prayer-sayer would stop in front of the ancient elm tree to examine the lists of death announcements pinned to the tree trunk. I noticed him shaking his head in disappointment when there were no Jewish deaths. "So, another day without an extra few lei," he appeared to say to himself. (He did get paid for his prayers!)

Next to our room was an abandoned bathroom, which Laurence converted into a darkroom. He was thus able to see the quality of the pictures he had taken, and also to give some of the pictures to the people who had so graciously allowed him to capture their images. I did not take my notebook with me when we visited people's homes unless there was something very specific I wanted to record or draw, because the notebook intimidated people. The few life histories we recorded on tape were transcribed after we returned to the United States.

Today the Jews of Rădăuți think of themselves first as Jews, then as citizens of Romania. They do not consider themselves ethnically Romanian although they have adopted many aspects of the Romanian culture and behavior patterns. Likewise, other minority groups in Romania, such as Saxons, Swabians (of German origin), Hungarians, Serbs, Turks, Tartars, and Ukrainians, think of themselves first as members of their own ethnic and cultural groups. This separation of identity is further reflected in the use of language. Among themselves the Jews of Rădăuți speak either German or Yiddish, although they are able to speak fluent Romanian. Sometimes the Jews refer to Romanians as "Christians," especially when

The Main Temple of Rădăuți. The land on which it was erected was donated to the Jewish community by Emperor Franz Josef of Austria in the late nineteenth century.

they want to emphasize their non-Jewish identity. For instance, a Jew might talk about a person being married to a "Christian," meaning a Romanian. It seems that, to the Jews, religious affiliation rather than nationality is the most meaningful stamp on any Romanian's identity card.

Today Rădăuţi is a model town. It has new *bloculs* (block apartment houses) for people who have recently moved into town from the surrounding peasant communities to work at industrial jobs. Most of the cobblestone streets have been recently asphalted over; the small, individual stores left over from Austrian times in the town's center are scheduled to be demolished, to be replaced by the modern *bloculs*. Some of the remaining Jews are planning to emigrate soon; after that, in the words of one Jewish resident, the town will be *Judenrein*. All that will remain to show that Jews once lived and flourished there will be the few crumbling stones of the Jewish cemetery outside the town, next to a junkyard for cars.

The Last Jews of Rădăuţi

Religious Life

Laurence Salzmann

I grew up in a Jewish home in Philadelphia which, over the years, became less and less Jewish in the traditional sense. Perhaps this was due to the deaths of my grandmothers when I was quite young. I remember them lighting the *Shabbes* candles; with their passing, *Shabbes* was no longer celebrated in our home. My mother had been brought up in the Reform Jewish Movement, which I have come to consider something of a Jewish church. She did not carry on the *Shabbes* tradition.

When I came of age for my Bar Mitzva, I remember spending long, arduous hours with my father, learning to read and recite the Hebrew portion of the Torah and the prayers. My father had little patience with my learning and often would smack me if I didn't get the lessons right. I decided then and there that once my Bar Mitzva was over I did not want anything more to do with Jewish learning. The day after my Bar Mitzva I stopped attending Sunday School.

Going to live with the Jewish community of Rădăuţi brought me once again in contact with a Jewish way of life. I came to appreciate and celebrate the yearly cycle of Jewish holidays and rituals, and became part of a community of Jews and their customs. I discovered aspects of my faith that I had never practiced or seen at home (such as the practices relating to the preparation of a corpse for burial). The Jews of Rădăuţi used to say to me, "*Du bist einer von unsers*" (You are one of us).

After returning from Rădăuți I attended Yom Kippur services at one of Philadelphia's largest synagogues. I felt a certain anonymity in being a member of this synagogue, to which my family belonged. In Rădăuți, one's presence in the synagogue was very much felt—in fact it was essential. Often there was just barely the minyan (ten men) that was needed for the services to begin.

I regularly attended services at the Wiznitzer Shul. The members, half jokingly, called me the Wiznitzer *Chasid*—a *Chasid* is a follower of some learned rabbi. The Wiznitzer Shul had been established in Rădăuți by the followers of the great, learned rabbi of Wiznitz, a town in the Ukraine. His family had established synagogues all over Eastern Europe, where the congregants prayed according to the traditions and style set forth by him and his family.

In Rădăuți there were still two functioning small prayer houses referred to as shuls, the Wiznitzer and the Chessed Shel Emeth. In addition, there was the main synagogue called the Main Temple. Not long ago there had been twenty-three different prayer houses, each with its own congregation and rabbi. The congregants sometimes represented different class structures and professional groups. For example, the tailors and shoemakers had their own special shul. Vestiges of this voluntarily imposed segregation could be seen at the *Shabbes* services that I attended at the Wiznitzer Shul: one Friday evening in March of 1975 I observed that the attendants included a shoemaker, a barber, a frame maker, a glass cutter, a fur hat maker, a fur coat maker, two ex-farmers, an ex-wood dealer, a professional kaddish

---

The old Hebrew prayer books at the Wiznitzer Shul. Eventually, they will be burned according to Jewish tradition, when there are no more congregants of the shul living.

Men reading in silence on a Friday night at the Wiznitzer Shul.

Simon Tessler—in the fifties he was sentenced by the State to five years of hard labor. His crime was to take a spool of thread from the textile factory where he had been working. No wonder he used to say, "You must have luck in your job."

Mr. Lehrer carrying the Torah of the Wiznitzer Shul.

Kiddush after the Saturday morning service.

sayer, two retired Jewish Committee functionaries, a mattress maker, and a photographer—myself.

Mr. Moses Lehrer, as the cohen, conducted the services at the Wiznitzer Shul, which was open only for Friday evening and Saturday morning prayers. He also acted as the shul's *gabbai* (caretaker)—if a window was broken or a door needed fixing, he repaired it. His wife, Zile, baked the cakes, which were served with a little bit of shnaps after the Saturday morning service.

Friday night services at the Wiznitzer Shul were very special: the men would come a little earlier, sitting in the small sanctuary where the services were to be held (the larger one was more costly to heat, so it was used only during summer months). They warmed themselves by the crackling of the woodburning stove (made out of an old oil drum) and talked in hushed tones, in small groups. A real feeling of camaraderie existed among those who came to pray at the Wiznitzer Shul. Sometimes it was necessary for Mr. Lehrer to send out for an extra man or two if the minyan was not complete; he borrowed men from the nearby Chessed Shel Emeth.

After the Friday evening services Moses Lehrer would look outside for a passing Romanian, for he needed a Christian to turn off the shul's lights, which had been turned on before the Sabbath had begun.

No women were present at the shul; they came to the synagogue only for the more important holidays. They would sit apart from the men, up in the balcony, which was an enclosed space and allowed them to peer down only from behind the glass partitions.

Often after Friday services I would walk Abraham Kern to his home. We would meet the other men coming from Chessed Shel, and a *Gut Shabbes* greeting would be exchanged.

The Wiznitzer Shul will not stay open much longer. All the men who go to pray there are well on in age. The sons of these men do not follow in their fathers' footsteps, and soon there will be no one to open the doors

9

on *Shabbes* evenings and no one to light the stove and the candles. The few remaining worshipers will continue their prayers at the main temple, across from the market square. And the shul, because of its location on a residential street, will probably become the home of a Romanian family who will not even know who the Wiznitzer *rebbe* was.

During all the time I was in Rădăuţi, contrary to the accepted Jewish practices, I was allowed to photograph most of the religious ceremonies in the synagogue and small prayer houses. The only person to object was Pinchas Mencher, the ritual prayer sayer, whose objections were overruled by the larger community.

A non-Jewish Romanian woman is turning off the lights at the Main Temple after the Saturday services. (On the Sabbath, Jews do not engage in tasks which require physical labor.)

Clipper's Bar Mitzva

Only one Bar Mitzva took place in the twenty months we were in Rădăuţi, that of Willie Clipper of Brodina, a small town close to Rădăuţi. For many months we watched Willie preparing for this event with a conscientiousness that matched Rabbi Tirnauer's. The rabbi was Willie's devoted tutor. Willie would come each Sunday afternoon and sit with him in his study; the boy was learning Hebrew and studying the relevant prayers for his Bar Mitzva. We were often visitors at the rabbi's house, and on one of those occasions Laurence was able to take these photographs.

When we were in Rădăuţi there were very few young people left, perhaps no more than twenty or twenty-five. They all attended Romanian schools, and a good number of them were enrolled in universities to acquire skills or train for professions that they would be able to use when they left Romania. Almost none of the young men and women planned to stay in Romania after completing their studies.

Up until ten years ago there were classes in Yiddish for Jewish students attending high school. These classes are no longer offered—there are too few Jews. Instead, an informal *hader* is conducted by Irwin Rosenbaum, a retired businessman-scholar, who teaches Jewish children Hebrew and Jewish lore on Sunday mornings.

Willie came to an early morning service at the synagogue on his Bar Mitzva day. Like all observant Jewish males, he put on his tefillin (small leather boxes containing scriptures, which are strapped to the forehead and left arm, symbolizing recognition and worship of God).

Later, he was called on to read a section from the Torah, thus demonstrating publicly his knowledge and understanding of tefillin and his ability to pray in Hebrew. These rites completed, he was confirmed a man. After the service Willie's mother handed out pieces of cake that she had baked and his father poured out the shnaps he had brought for the congregants' toast to the Bar Mitzva boy.

Willie Clipper, flanked by his father and the rabbi, is putting on tefillin.

Willie with Rabbi Tirnauer in his study, preparing for his Bar Mitzva.

Brith Milah

Abraham Kern used to complain to me about his son Isaac, who had married a non-Jew—a fact that saddened Abraham. But when Isaac's wife bore a son, Abraham was very cooperative in arranging for the grandson's Brith Milah. Invited to the Kerns' house for this occasion were the fellow congregants of the Wiznitzer Shul, as well as the rabbi, who also acted as *mohel,* and the president of the Jewish Committee seen on the opposite page, holding the infant wrapped in the bunting, while Rabbi Tirnauer is preparing to say the blessings.

Strictly speaking, according to Jewish law, a child is considered Jewish only if the mother is Jewish; technically, therefore, David Kern was not entitled to the Brith Milah ritual. However, no one seemed to consider this fine point of Jewish law. Why? Probably because, with so few Jewish children being born to Jewish parents, it mattered little to the last Jews of Rădăuţi that David was not Jewish. What really mattered was that both his father and his grandfather wanted him to begin life according to Jewish traditions, and the community acquiesced to their desire for a Brith Milah for the young Kern.

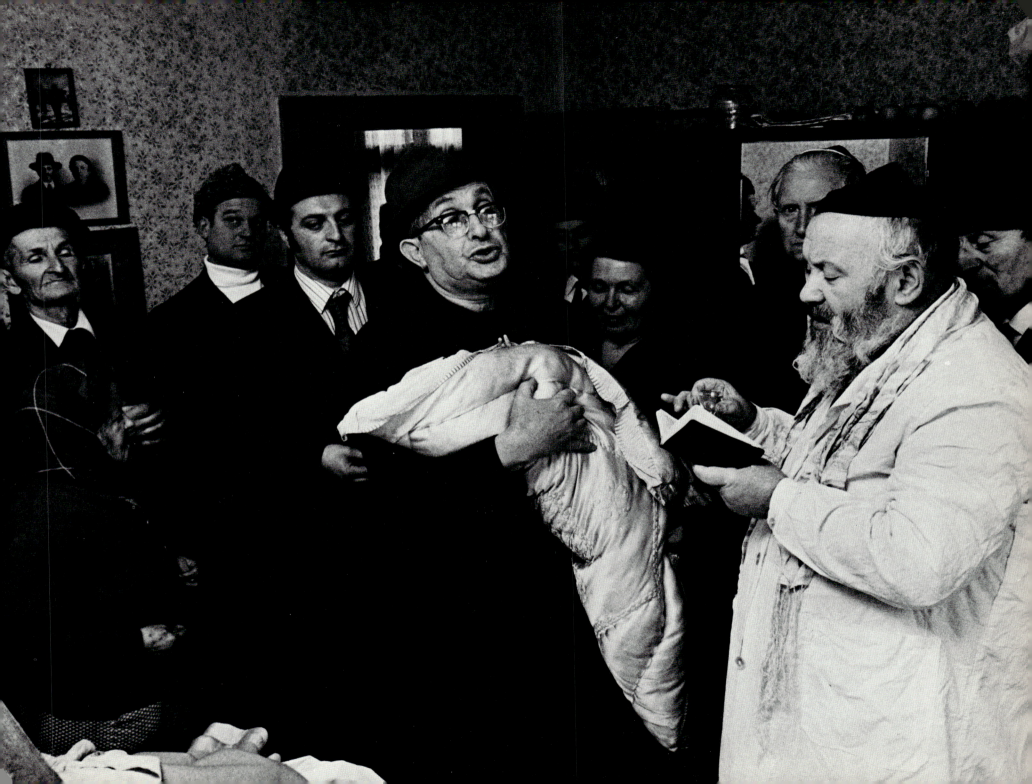

Women

Frau Weinstein

"When one has luck, one lives," said Frau Weinstein as she settled down in her chair after serving us coffee and cognac. Just as she was preparing to tell us some of her recollections, her ailing mother seated herself next to her, as a witness to the past. Frau Weinstein's face had traces of long years of hardship; her eyes were gentle and kind. As the wife of the bookkeeper of the Jewish Committee, she led a quiet, modest life; her major concerns were the futures of her son and daughter, who were both students of mathematics at the University of Iasi.

In 1941 Frau Weinstein had entered a concentration camp at Kopaigorod as an eighteen-year-old girl. She vividly remembers standing in line with the other young, able-bodied men and women, waiting to be picked out for labor camps:

> A German officer came and ordered us to go to a nearby forest. There we were organized to stand in rows. He began with the men, picking out those who were seemingly healthy and could work. My brother was among those selected. I was small and weak, and was afraid that the officer wouldn't take me and that I would remain there

Frau Weinstein makes the blessing over the Friday night Shabbes candles.

and die. Suddenly I ran over to the group where my brother was standing with the other selected people. Surprisingly, the German officer and the Romanian soldier didn't say anything to me, and I was saved. A little later, another girl decided to do the same as I did and the German officer shot her. He had only wounded her and she was crying "Mama, Mama," so he went up to her and shot her again. The German officer then said that each person selected out could choose someone left behind. My brother chose my father, and I, my mother. So the whole family was out. Then we were sent back to the little town, where we were ghettoized. The others remained in the forest, where they died.

Their sojourn in the camp lasted until 1944, when the Russians set them free.

She said that in those three years she grew up very fast:

When the war broke out in 1939 I was just sixteen and hadn't really lived. I had my small circle of friends; we used to get together Saturday afternoons and dance to music from the radio. This lasted only a short while. . . . At the camp I had a very serious case of bronchitis. After I recovered I took a small walk one day to the center of the ghetto. The sight was horrifying. In front of a house stood a wagon. They were throwing corpses into it, just like one would throw a dog, until the wagon was full. I vomited and fainted, right where I was standing. Luckily, some neighbors came and carried me away.

The interior of the Weinstein house was neat and simple, filled with flowers and direct light, which entered from a glass-enclosed porch. The environment, in fact, reflected a certain peacefulness in Mrs. Weinstein that was derived from her contentment with her present circumstances.

Frau Weinstein with her mother.

Schecter Sisters

In Rădăuţi one often found unmarried or widowed sisters and brothers living together. The brothers would provide for the household while the sisters made a comfortable nest for all. In a sense these people were husbands and wives.

The two Schecter sisters lived together in a two-room apartment. When Laurence and I walked into their living room, the older sister, Mali, was polishing the *Shabbes* candlesticks. She did not want Laurence to take her picture, saying that they lived poorly and did not want their home exposed to the public through photographs.

We spoke with Lotti Schecter, the younger sister; she volunteered to show us her picture album. One photograph was of a Mr. Klein, who had asked her to marry him. She had loved him but did not "accept his hand in marriage," because she did not want to leave her family in Rădăuţi and move to Chile with him. That was before the war. During the war, her experiences at the camp in Transnistria (in the Ukraine) were very painful; her entire family died except for a brother and Mali. After the war Lotti and Mali returned to Rădăuţi to continue their humble existence.

When Laurence returned to Rădăuţi in 1979, he found the following inscription on Lotti Schecter's tombstone:

Wenn Liebe konte Wunder tun
und Tränen die Toten wecken,
Dann wurde dich,
meine treue Schwester,
nicht schon die kuhle
Erde decken.

Deine introstliche Schwester

If love could make miracles
if tears could bring back the dead
then, you
my true sister
would not be covered by the cool earth.

Your inconsolable sister

Relly Blei

Relly Blei is a poet and an intellectual, fluent in Yiddish, German, and French. In fact, she has translated some of her Yiddish poems into German. Her books have been published by a Romanian publishing house that specializes in books on ethnic cultures and languages.*

When I first met her, I was struck by her great enthusiasm for literature. The bookshelves were filled with Russian, German, and French classics. She cited from Goethe, Gogol, Dante, Hugo, and Proust effortlessly, drawing inspiration from them to explain the vicissitudes of human existence. During the course of our conversation, however, we managed to touch upon more personal matters, her own poetry and her activities as an educated woman in the 1930s.

She spoke clearly, choosing her words with care and delicacy, as she recalled her youthful involvement with the political and intellectual movement of the 1930s in Romania. At the time she had been a dedicated and active member of the Jewish Youth Movement against Fascism. In

---

* Her latest books are entitled: *Lieder* (1966), *De-A Lungal Anilor* (1976), *Frauen Alcik* (1980), *Clipe de tristete, clipe fericite* (1982), all published by Editura Kriterion, Bucuresti.

25

Relly Blei lending books from her library to a friend.

1936–37, when she was in Paris studying literature, she had joined anti-fascist demonstrations.

On her return to Rădăuţi from Paris in the late 1930s, she and her husband continued their protests along with many of their friends. Her sister, her brother, and a close friend were imprisoned for their anti-fascist activities. Some of the young Jewish intellectuals in their circle went to fight in Spain.

During this period the Romanian Iron Guardists were beginning to set up pogroms in the big cities. In Iasi and Bucharest Jews were slaughtered and hung from meat hooks. When Cernauti was ceded to Russia in 1940 many young Jews, including Relly Blei and her husband, fled there to escape from the Romanian fascists. Soon World War II broke out. Relly Blei's entire family (thirty people) were deported to camps in Transnistria. She was parted from her husband, who was mobilized in the Russian army. They were not to see each other for the next four years.

Her accounts of life at camps were chilling; occasionally she'd read from a poem to convey an emotional state, a personal revolt, moments of desperation that transformed into episodes of tenderness. In a poem entitled "Convoy" she wrote of her forced wanderings from one camp to another:

One December morning, around six o'clock, the gendarmes came to the house where we had been staying. My son was only a few months old. They took us about fifteen kilometers to another place, with the gendarmes following us. Old people stayed on the side of the road and froze to death. A woman had to leave her child behind because she couldn't carry him. They took us to an old schoolhouse, without a door or windows. There, I saw dead people on the floor. It was late at night. I preferred to sit outside and die rather than sit inside with the dead. An old Ukrainian man came, took me to his house,

Relly Blei, a nationally known Yiddish poet, has been able to create an intellectual environment for her friends, Jew and Romanian alike.

and told his wife that he had brought home a "guest." They prepared a bed for me. They were extraordinary people. Another friend of theirs who was with a child asked me if she could nurse my son. I was so happy that she would do it. I stayed at their house for two weeks. Then the gendarmes came again and would not let Jews stay with Ukrainian families. The Ukrainian woman was very compassionate; she told me how to escape. That's how I survived.

The meeting with her estranged husband was in Chernovtsy. She said, "my husband was a very handsome, elegant man. But many days had to pass for me to be with the man to whom I had said good-bye four years ago."

He has been dead for over ten years now. Despite this great loss, Relly Blei pursues her literary career as ardently as ever. She divides much of her time between visiting her son in Germany and staying with her sister in Bucharest, where she attends conferences annually. The summer months are spent in her small, orderly apartment in Rădăuți, writing.

Both her poetry and prose are testimonies to a strong commitment to the "ideal socialist state" and love of mankind. She seemed to appreciate the economic advantages of the present socialist regime in Romania. She emphasized the absence of anti-Semitism in Romania today; at least it was "not part of the 'official party policy' "; all children, Romanian and Jewish alike, had equal rights for education. The principal reason for the Jewish emigration to Israel in the fifties and sixties was the desire of Jewish people to "hold their head up and not feel discriminated against," she added. Personally, she has no desire to leave Romania. (She is one of the 30,000 Jews still living there.)

For twenty years before her retirement, when there were still a fair number of young Jewish students attending schools in Rădăuţi, Relly Blei had been a teacher of Yiddish in high school. After World War II she had helped establish a Jewish choir, and the repertory of songs included some of her poems set to music. She had also organized seminars on Jewish writers. As the past secretary of YKUF (International Jewish Cultural Organization, with its main offices in New York City), she still publishes in its literary journal.

The longer I spoke with her, the clearer it became why she had chosen to stay in Rădăuţi. On one hand she had very strong ties to Arbore, the nearby village where she was born. On the other hand, when she said, "I feel very tied to Romania," she was, in fact, expressing her pride at having been ideologically involved in the rebuilding of the Romanian state based on socialist principles. She had sown the seeds for the Jewish Youth Movement. Her early poems became metaphors for her visions of a unified, solid social system in Romania which, in the forties, was on the verge of collapse. Thus Relly Blei, the poet-intellectual-idealist, had generated a better life out of her own higher consciousness, and was continuing to do so by inspiring and educating her fellow Jews and Romanians.

She is a person transformed, I believe, above and beyond ethnic and religious boundaries. She is a universal person.

Four Poems of Relly Blei
translated by Max Rosenfeld

MY SHTETL

I still can see my little native town
Old and stooped and dirty.
Its narrow unpaved streets
Deprived of any mark of beauty.

After every rain the town
Became a sea of mud.
At night the darkness hid it
from the moon's pale glow.

I felt so sorry for my little town—
Sleepy, sad and plain.
I dreamed some day I'd leave it—
But that's where I remained.

Now, after all these years
I'm full of envy of my shtetl.
I have aged—but she's grown younger.
Will she tell me what her secret is?

In her old age she's begun to grow,
Straightened up her back, reaches for the sun.
Pretties herself with finery and flowers
Appropriate for the young.

She's decked herself in verdant ribbons
Covered her mud with stone and brick.
Erected shining neon lights
So she can promenade after dark.

Her work improves from day to day
Her blocks of homes are bright and pretty.
My little town: I wish you luck—
May you grow up to be a city!

מיין שטעטל

ס'שטייט פאר מיר מיין שטעטל פון צוריק מיט מיט יארן
אלט און איינגעהויקערט, קוויטיק און פארשטויבט.
מיט די שמאלע געסלער אן קיין טראטוארן,
ס'איז געווען מיין שטעטל פון אלץ וואס שיין, באריבט.

ס'פלעגן אויף די גאסן שטענדיק נאך א רעגן
כוואליען זיך די בלאטעס, גלאנצן ווי א טייך,
און ביינאכט איז חושך איבער אים נעלעגן
ס'האט נאר די לבנה עס באלויכטן בלייך.

כ'האב געהאט רחמנות אויף מיין אלטן שטעטל
וואס געווען פארשלאפן, אומעטיק און פוסט.
כ'האב געחלומט שטענדיק איך זאל עס פארבייטן
נאר אין אים פארבלייבן האב איך דאך געמוזט.

איצט נאך לאנגע יארן איז געשען א וווּנדער,
בין איך זי מקנא איצט מיין אלטע שטאט.
איך בין אלט געוואָרן, זי ווערט שענער, יונגער
וועט זי מיר אנטפלעקן פון דעם נס דעם סוד?

זי האט אויך דער עלטער אנגעהויבן וואקסן
גלייכט זיך אויס איר פלייצע, שטרעקט זיך צו דער זון
צירט זי זיך מיט בלומען ווי עס פאסט פאר יונגע
און אין נייע קליידער זי האט זיך אנגעטאָן.

זי האט ארומגעגארטלט זיך מיט גרינע בענדער,
זי האט די בלאטעס אירע אונטער שטיין פארמאכט.
האט זי אנגעצונדן ווייסע נעאנליכטער,
זי זאל זיך באווייזן קענען אויך באנאכט.

ס'וואקסן אירע בלאקן הויכע און העלע
זע איך ווי ווי די די ארבעט בעסער אלץ געראָט.
ווינטש איך איר מיין שטאט, זי זאל ווייטער וואקסן
און זי זאל איינגיכן זיין א גרויסע שטאט.

MY FRIENDS

It is late autumn and I am all alone.
I have tried to walk away from myself.
But where to, when the wind whips the branches
And they smack you angrily in the face?
When the gray sky sheds rivers of tears
And the yellow leaves swirl around in the dust.
I am all alone, tired of saying nothing
But weary of writing still another sad poem.
I need to be comforted so I won't fall ill.

And then my bookcase on the wall
Reaches out and welcomes me with open arms
As though I were a guest just entering
And now I am no longer all alone.
No longer do I hear the heavens weep—
My friend is entertaining me with stories—
His lovely smile makes everything seem right.
So once again, accept my gratitude—
My faithful friends, my old familiar books.

מיינע פריינט

ס׳איז שפּעטער האַרבסט. אין שטוב איך בין אַליין.
כ׳האָב שוין געפֿרווט פֿון זיך אויעקצוגיין.
ווּ גייט מען עס אַז ווינט די צווייגן רייסט,
און זיי מיט צאָרן ריר אין פּנים שמייסט?
— אַז גרויער הימל מייכן טרערן גיסט —
אַז געלע בלעטער וואַלגערן זיך אין מיסט.
איך בין אַליין. פֿון שוויייגן כ׳בין שוין מיר —
אויך מיר צי שרייבן נאָך אַ מרוירי
ק ליד.
איך זוך אַ טרייסט איך זאָל ניט ווערן קראַנק,

און איך דערזע — מיין אַלטן ביכערשראַנק.
אַ גרויסן, ברייטן שלום גיט ער מיר,
ווי פֿאַר אַ גאַסט ער עפֿנט אויף די טיר.
און איצט — אין שטוב איך בין נישט מער אַליין,
איך הער נישט מער פֿון הימל דאָס געוויין.
אַ שיינע מעשׂה מיר דערצייַלט אַ פֿריינט —
זײַן ליבער שמייכל אַלצדינג העל באַשײַנט.
דערפֿאַר איך זאָג אײַך נאָכאַמאָל: מיין דאַנק
איר ליבע פֿריינט פֿון אַלטן ביכער שראַנק.

33

SILENCE

I said a word.
You misunderstood.
Silence spread between us.
Still, we were together.
I shared your pain
Along with all your joys.
And when the silence grew too much for me
When your pride kept you mute
I felt your heart beat close to mine.
Your eye caressed me tenderly
And soon the clouds dispersed.
Once again you told me everything.

And now you're silent, forever silent.
And forever I'll be longing for your voice.

שווייגן

איך האָב געזאָגט א וואָרט —
דו האָסט עס פאלש פארשטאנען —
און צווישן אונדז ס׳האָט שווייגן זיך געשפרייט.
נאָר כ׳בין געווען אויך דאן מיט דיר צוזאמען.
געווייטיקט כ׳האָב מיט דיר
און זיך מיט דיר געפרייט.
און ווען ס׳איז שווער געוואָרן מיר די שטילקייט,
און דו אין שטאָלץ דיינעם האָסט נישט גערעדט,
איך האָב געפילט דאָם הארץ דיינם גאָענט קלאפן
און ס׳האָט דיין אויג מיט ליבשאפט מיך געגלעט.
דאָך באלד די כמאַרעס האָבן זיך פארצויגן,
האָסט אַלץ דערצײַלט מיר ווידער ווי אמאל —

און איצט דו שווייַנסט — וועסט אייביק, אייביק שווייַגן
און אייביק וועל איך בענקען נאָך דײַן קול.

IN BEYLA'S CELLAR

Driven into this little town
I stand abandoned in the street.
The cold wind penetrates my bones
And my child is almost frozen.

Shadows fall upon the earth,
Dark and fearful is the night.
I beg, I plead, at every door,
But they are all shut tight.

A beggar finally takes pity
On my child, perhaps on me
And leads us both to Beyla's cellar
Where the door is always open.

On the floor lie rows of people
Huddling close together.
Beneath a table in the corner
Sleeps a human being.

Snow and mud their pillows,
The frosty wind their quilt,
Blowing in through every crack—
And this is where my child must rest.

Though I now believed in nothing
Here a miracle took place.
For the first time in his life
My son has called me Mama.

For the first time in my life
I heard that wondrous word,
The word that brought me joy and strength
The word that was my only solace.

In the muddy snow
I sat beside my child,
Bent my weary head to his
As my tears washed his hands

I forgot where we were sitting,
That bugs were walking on the floor.
I forgot it was the dead of winter
That tomorrow I'd be in the street.

New hope was born within me
My heart felt lighter, cleansed.
I was not deserted, lost, alone:
I had a son who'd take revenge!

(Written in the Ghetto of Transnistria)

ביי ביילען אין קיילער

אין א שטעטל ווו איך בין פארטריבן
שטיי איך אויף דער גאס, אליין, פארלוירן.
ס׳גייט א קאַלטער ווינט מיר דורך די ביינער
און איך זע: מײַן קינד איז באלד פארפרוירן.

שוין עס לאָזן זיך אראָף די שאָטנס,
שוין עס קומט מיט שרעק די שוואַרצע נאכט,
און איך בעט זיך, בעט בײַ אלע טירן
נאָר זיי בלײַבן אלע פעסט פארמאכט.

ס׳האָט א בעטלער פארט געחאָט רחמונות
אויף מײַן קינד, און אפשר אויך אויף מיר,
האָט ער מיך געפירט צו ביילעס קיילער —
דאָרט עס האָט געעפנט זיך די טיר.

אויפן דיל עס ליגן מענטשן, מענטשן,
איינער צו דעם אנדערן צוגעדריקט.
אין א ווינקל שטייט א קלייטנשיק טישל,
אונט ערן טישל אויכעט איינער ליגט.

שניי און בלאָטע זענען זייערע קישן,
צודעק איז דער פראָסט, דער קאַלטער ווינט
וואָס ער בלאָזט ארײַן פון אלע שפאַרעס,
ליגן דאָרט האָט אויך געמוזט מײַן קינד.

כאַטש איך קען אין גאָרנישט מער שוין גלויבן
עס געשען א ווונדער נאָר מסתּמא:
דאָרטן האָט צום ערשטן מאָל אין לעבן
מיר מײַן קינד גערופן: מאמע!

דאָרט האָב איך צום ערשטן מאָל אין לעבן
א דאָס טײַערע וואָרט געהערט
וואָס עס האָט מיר גליק און טרייסט געגעבן
און האָט מיר די כּוחות פארמערט.

האָב איך אין דעם שניי און אין דער בלאָטע
צו דעם קינד מײַנעם זיך צוגעזעצט,
האָב מײַן מידן קאָפ צו אים געבויגן
און מיט טרערן זײַנע הענטעלעך באנעצט.

כ׳האָב פארגעסן ווו כ׳האָב מיך געפונען
און אז אויפן דיל שפאַצירן זיך די לײַז.
כ׳האָב פארגעסן אז ס׳איז קאַלטער ווינטער
און אז מאָרגן בין איך אויף דער גאס.

ס׳האָט א האָפענונג זיך אין מיר צעוועקסן
ס׳איז אין הארץ געוואָרן ליכטיק, רייַן:
— דו ביסט נישט אליין, פארלאָזט, פארלוירן,
דו האָסט א זון וואָס וועט זיך נוקם זיין!

אין געטא טראנסניסטריען

Fräulein Grünglas

One day I met Fräulein Grünglas at the supermarket. She resembled a little bird flitting along the sidewalk with no wings. Who would have known that she spoke perfect English, in addition to French, Russian, German, and Yiddish?

Several weeks later Laurence and I rang her doorbell; no one answered. Some neighbors across the street said they could never tell if she was home. I peeked through the window and could see her leaning over a pile of things. I knocked on the glass. She finally opened the door with a toothless smile that discouraged me from going in. I said I wished to talk to her and that Laurence was also going to take a few pictures. Then she allowed us in.

We were in a semidark room; there were several sofas piled with clothes and newspapers, a wardrobe, a round table, and many, many bundles of old letters and photographs on a table near the window and strewn about the floor. Did she keep an untidy house, or was she on the verge of moving? Then I saw a couple of steamer trunks addressed to herself, but lacking destination.

It was getting darker inside; a chicken flew in through the half-opened door. Fräulein Grünglas, clearly embarrassed about the disorder, covered her mouth with one hand while digging nervously through the clothes pile. "I look worse than a grandmother," she added, referring to her missing teeth and shabby clothes. We tried to assure her that she looked fine, and asked her if she could tell us a little bit about her life. Where was she born, did she have any relatives, where was she sending the steamer trunks?

She had relatives everywhere—Israel, Germany, Cleveland, New York; her brother and sister visited her occasionally, but in Rădăuţi she was alone. Photographs of cousins in Cleveland, letters from a brother in Israel, provided her with momentary comforts. Yet she was unable to separate herself from her memories, which seemed to be buried alive in the dark recesses of her room.

"A swallow doesn't make a spring, and I am just one little bird." Thus she described her lonely life.

As a young woman she had been the manager of a clothing factory. Her family had lived in Chernovtsy, forty miles away, which was once considered to be the cultural center of Bukovina (many people in Rădăuţi came from Chernovtsy). Some of her faded photographs showed her skiing with various boyfriends; in the end, she had married no one. She was detained in Romania when she was in her early thirties; she remained silent about the reasons. Did she enjoy being single, or had she not found her proper match? Was the current regime punishing her for her connections with key people in the previous government? Though reticent, she did mention that the rest of her family had been permitted to leave.

Fräulein Grünglas once asked me in perfect English, "Do you know what life is?"

Fräulein Grünglas during one of those rare moments
when she agreed to pose for a photograph.

She was living on a very small pension from the government. Her
brother, who had been a very skilled jeweler in Rădăuţi, had recently
come back from Israel to stay with her. But then he was picked up by the
Romanian militia and sent back to Israel. (Once one leaves the country,

it is very difficult to come back, except as a visitor.) She pointed at her tiny pearl earrings, made by her brother. She could never understand why we were asking her questions about herself, and why Laurence was clicking the camera as she coyly smiled or crossed her arms across her chest. "I don't know you, why are you taking my picture? Tell me, are you a philosopher, do you know what life is?" After a few moments of silence, she added, "Life is a laugh and a tear."

Then, getting up from the edge of her cluttered bed, she gave out a short laugh and walked outside to the chicken coop in the front yard to collect the solitary warm egg that her winged companion had laid for the day.

Families

The Tirnauers

Rabbi Tirnauer was one of the first people Laurence met when he went to the early morning services in Rădăuţi. He was a venerable man, well liked by both the Romanian and Jewish communities. When he was not performing his duties in the synagogue, in the butcher shop, or at the cemetery, he was at home reading or listening to people who sought his advice, Christians and Jews alike. As the rabbi of Rădăuţi and a few other neighboring towns, he spent three days a week traveling on local buses. His wife and daughter worried about his exhausting trips and would hover over him when he arrived home. Once in a while the rabbi could not get back home on the expected day because of too much snow on the roads, and Bertha, his daughter, would quietly reassure her mother that he was safer staying in the village than coming home.

Josef Tirnauer—as the sole rabbi of the Bukovina region, he officiated at many religious functions. He was also sought out by Christians for advice.

Portrait of Rabbi Tirnauer's parents, occupying a central place on the wall of their living room.

The rabbi at Chanuka, lighting the candles of the menorah.

Bertha was the only daughter of the Tirnauer family.

Several months after Laurence had made his acquaintance, the rabbi invited us to his home to meet his wife and daughter. Their modest, one-story house was located on the main street leading to the synagogue. The Tirnauer family shared the house with the owners, the Wincklers, whose son had emigrated to Israel. We entered the house through an enclosed porch. The first room was the dining room, which doubled as the rabbi's study. Here there were glass-enclosed bookcases filled with prayer books. On top of them were silver wine cups and many, many menorahs, candle-holders, and other memorabilia, including faded photographs of the rabbi's first wife and children. The study led to the guest room, where the family also slept at night. When we came in, the Rabbi was sitting at the table, reading his prayer books; he looked up, nodded politely, continued with his prayers. Even at home the Rabbi socialized little, not engaging in casual conversation. He was known to be a loner. His family tiptoed around him.

The rabbi was born in 1913 near Oradea, a city in Transylvania. He had spent nine years in a yeshiva in Satu Mare and later studied with Rabbi Mendel Harger in Viscus de Sus. As part of his rabbinical training, he had learned to become a *shochet,* a ritual slaughterer; he was extremely busy in this role.

He was twenty-seven years of age at the outbreak of the war. By the end of it he had lost every member of his family and had developed diabetes and a heart disease. He remained a widower for quite a while before he married Bertha's mother. Despite the tragedies he had experienced, he was a kind man with a biting sense of humor. He always started his life history by saying, "I was born poor; my wife and children were killed in Auschwitz. I am fine now. . . ." He never talked about his ailments, nor intimated his feelings; there was almost an invisible shield around his person.

His second wife, Esther, took very good care of him and looked up to him all through their marriage. She was a highly religious woman who was very proud of her kosher kitchen; even the Romanian maid had been taught its intricacies. Once Mr. Winckler told us that the rabbi and his family had never come to dinner in all the twelve years they'd lived as neighbors because the Wincklers were not "kosher enough" for the Tirnauers.

Esther Tirnauer's eyes were almost invisible behind the thick lenses of her glasses. She tilted her head back when she talked and assumed an expression that was a mixture of the serious and the melancholic. She was, in fact, a perfect match for Rabbi Tirnauer, and had also been born in Oradea.

They shared a common language, Hungarian. But Yiddish was the spoken language between them, for she spoke very little Romanian. When we visited them at home, Mrs. Tirnauer would open the door (if Bertha, their twenty-one-year-old daughter, was not at home) and tell us that Bertha was out. I think that implied a certain kind of reluctance to be with us; she was more willing to join us when Bertha was there. Then we would be served rich, Hungarian-style pastries and coffee. We discussed daily events, births, deaths, and restrictions imposed by the state upon purchasing consumer goods and traveling abroad. Bertha helped Laurence with his Romanian, and also helped us understand the custom of doing and receiving *favors*, a traditional method through which a lot can be accomplished without having to go through the bureaucracy of the state. Bertha's drive to emigrate to Israel was a recurrent topic of conversation.

The Tirnauers would take us into the living room, where we sat on large, comfortable sofas (which were used as beds). Bertha also prepared her lessons there. She taught at a high school several kilometers from Rădăuţi and came home only on weekends; the weekdays were spent in

The rabbi as the shochet.

the home of a Christian Romanian family, who looked upon her as their eldest daughter and respected her as a teacher and an educated person. She was almost a celebrity to them. They were her family away from home; even *we* were invited to their home for a lavish lunch, as Bertha's guests.

Bertha's reasons for wanting to emigrate to Israel were clear: she wanted to be able to observe the Jewish Sabbath and holidays (as a teacher in a Romanian school, it was very hard to do so) and to continue her graduate studies in chemistry in a western accredited university. She also wanted to find a suitable Jewish mate—something next to impossible in Rădăuți. It took six months for her to get a visa. In the meantime she had been systematically preparing for her departure: buying furniture, crystal, linens, and even a fur hat, in case she lived in a cold region of Israel. When her furniture was sent in crates, her personal belongings were put in the small suitcase that she would take along with her on the plane.

The preparations for Bertha's trip saddened her mother, who was often in tears. She probably knew what Bertha knew, but avoided talking about it: that there was no coming back home. And there was little chance of the rabbi and Mrs. Tirnauer leaving Romania, since the rabbi was indispensable to the community. In contrast to his wife's uncontrolled tears over Bertha's departure, the rabbi displayed a great deal of control and charm. He would come into the house in his formal attire while the packing was going on, and would smile at us and say that "the capitalists" had "won over" his daughter. He never displayed publicly his feelings for his family. Rabbi Tirnauer had high hopes for his daughter. He loved her dearly but could not resolve the conflict between joining her in Israel and staying to serve his community and his people. He chose the latter. His wife, naturally, stayed with him.

The news of his death reached Bertha when she was in Jerusalem. The rabbi had died of a heart attack in the ambulance en route to the hospital. She was unable to get home in time for his funeral. (In order to leave

The rabbi and his daughter in front of their porch; this photo was taken a few months before Bertha left for Jerusalem.

Israel as a noncitizen and assure her return, she had to go through a lot of red tape that delayed her departure.) Eventually she did go back to Rădăuţi to console her ailing mother, who had no desire to stay in Romania anymore. (Several years after his death, the rabbi's body was taken to Israel for interment.)

Rabbi Tirnauer had provided his daughter with a very secure future, a good education, and a strong religious upbringing. He had encouraged her to leave for Israel and had paid for all the expenses of her emigration. (Even though her fare was paid by the Israeli government, Bertha had to "tip" many people to ensure getting the permit to leave on time.)

51

Bertha Tirnauer opening the gate for the Romanian woman who helped her mother to cook and clean every day.

The Rabbi by the Star of David monument, erected in memory of the Jews who never came back.

As the rabbi, he had consoled many, had given of himself to his congregation and even to the Christian Romanians who had asked for help. For about fifteen years he had conducted the ceremonies for every *brith*, marriage, and funeral in at least ten towns, including Rădăuţi. Laurence and I were not in Romania for his funeral, but we were told that large crowds of people paid their last respects to this man who smiled often and was kindly disposed to many. We still remember his earthy jokes. I always knew that he meant the opposite when he said: "Communism is *good*, you capitalists bring about ill-effects."

Several images of the rabbi are engraved in my memory: I see him walking rapidly along Strada Putnei toward the synagogue, with his wide-brimmed hat and his long black robe; chanting with his eyes closed and head tilted back at Friday evening services; and washing himself in the bathtub. That was a picture he liked a lot when Laurence showed it to him. It appealed to his sense of humor.

From the photo album of the Tirnauer family.

The Kerns

On Friday evenings Laurence used to walk home from the synagogue along the Strada Putnei with Abraham Kern, who insisted we come for *Shabbes* dinner. They'd stop at Abraham's shoe repair shop to pick up the *challa* Abraham had bought earlier. Then they would pick me up at the hotel. As we approached Mr. Kern's house, the *Shabbes* candles were glowing in the window; where we entered, his wife, Itta, had several traditional dishes cooking on the potbellied stove. Abraham would put the bread on the table and she'd cover it with a cloth. They'd call their son Isaac and his wife Leah in from their house in back and Abraham would pour out a little wine for everyone and then say a blessing over the wine and bread. Holding the *challa* against his ribs and slicing it toward himself, he'd cut off a piece of each of us. Handing it to us, his gesture said, "This is my bread, and I welcome you to share it and the camaraderie of *Shabbes* with us."

We got to know the Kerns especially well on these evenings. Compared to the other Jewish families the Kerns lived humbly. They had no running water; they got it from a communal well on the dirt road in front of their house. The parents' house was sparsely furnished and the floor was caving in. I felt that the war left them without the physical and emotional resources to care for their place. Isaac's house was better maintained—he

Abraham Kern.

Abraham Kern cutting his challa by candlelight on a *Shabbes* evening.

Abraham opened his shoe shop every morning and stayed there through the day, tinkering with a few repairs. His was a habit, a daily ritual.

The Passover table at the Kerns' home.

even had bottled gas in his kitchen. This convenience was also an inconvenience. When a bottle ran out Isaac or Leah would have to return it to the depot and might have to wait in line for six hours to get a new one.

Abraham said his life was a very sad one. As a Social Democrat in the thirties he had felt more brotherhood than he felt now, even though there was more poverty then. Today people did not seem to help each other the way they used to. Back then Itta had been preparing for a singing career and the famous Josef Schmidt had wanted her to go to Vienna to study with him. But her parents had not allowed her to go so she remained and married Abraham. She did not seem to regret the loss of an opera career, but did dwell on the hardships of their war experience.

She said that in the fall of 1941, around the time of the Jewish holidays, all the Jews were told to report to the railroad station and were put into railroad cars without being told where they were being taken.

They felt lucky that they didn't freeze to death, because it was a very cold winter. They were shipped part of the way in freight cars and had to continue by foot. One day as they were walking Itta got tired and sat down to rest. A soldier came up and told her to hurry on and leave her two-year-old Isaac behind. When she wouldn't leave him, the soldier struck her with his rifle, breaking her hand—which bothers her to this day. The family had a brief moment of reprieve when they were taken in and hidden by some Russian peasants, but eventually they arrived at Transnistria, where they were ghettoized and put to forced labor. During their four years there both Itta's parents died. Abraham, who said he had been a poor child who "always had to go around looking for work just to have a piece of bread to eat," particularly remembers the starvation in Transnistria. He suffered many illnesses and injuries from which he never recovered. Isaac was so undernourished that his bones grew crooked and he had to have special therapy for a year. Fortunately he grew up without any deformities.

When the Kerns returned to Rădăuţi, only the brick walls of their house were standing. Firewood had been so scarce during the war that all the doors and windows and other woodwork had been taken. Shortages of materials made reconstruction of the house very difficult.

Abraham Kern was able to return to his previous line of work. He had his own shoe repair shop and was able to continue running it as an independent business. When we met him he was too feeble to do much business, but he spent many hours each day in his shop, which was now his sacred domain.

Like most of the Jewish families of Rădăuţi, the Kerns had only one child, in whom they placed all their hopes for a better life. Isaac grew up with high ambitions and went off to the University of Bucharest with the hope of becoming an electrical engineer. He fell short of this ambition but became a successful TV repairman and returned to Rădăuţi.

After the birth of their son David, Isaac and Leah began thinking of moving to Israel. Isaac wanted his son to be brought up in a traditional Jewish way and did not want him to have the same experience he had had. Isaac told us, "My great-grandfather was born in Rădăuţi, my grandfather was born in Rădăuţi, my father was born in Rădăuţi, I was born in Rădăuţi, and my son was born in Rădăuţi. However, if my son wants to be an officer or an airman or to have a diplomatic career, they will say that he's a Jew and cannot."

Like many Romanians, Christian and Jewish alike, Isaac suffered from the pervasive restrictions that regulated his life. One of these restrictions was against free enterprise, which made Isaac's moonlighting TV repair service illegal. He was able to get many private customers who were willing to pay extra to have him do their repairs more quickly and better than

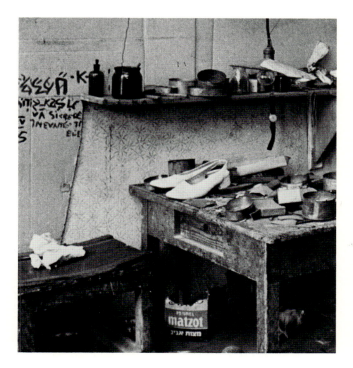

Abraham Kern's wooden workbench, cluttered with hand-tools, repair materials, and very few shoes to repair.

61

they would have done at the state-owned shop where he worked. He could make almost as much doing the private repairs as he could on his regular job. But he could not spend this money conspicuously for fear the authorities would confiscate it. As the family prepared to leave for Israel this money came in handy, but it had to be used in accordance with other restrictions. Emigrants can take no money out of the country, but they are allowed to take the equivalent of one roomful of furniture per person. Since household goods are very expensive in Israel, Romanian emigrants moving there take their full quota of furniture with them. Isaac's extra money went largely into buying and shipping household possessions for his family's new life. At this point the Kerns became consumer oriented for the first time in their lives. Like Bertha Tirnauer, they had to give "tips" to civil servants for getting permits through faster and getting allowances for excess baggage. The Kerns expected to get a large sum of money for their house but were disappointed: the government, to which they were obligated to sell it, gave them only one quarter of its value.

Additional unpleasant treatment accompanied the family's departure for Israel. Emigrants were not allowed to take any of the following items with them when they left: prayer books, icons, and other religious articles; personal letters, photographs, and documents of an official nature; paintings, antiques, and jewelry other than a watch and a wedding band. They were thus stripped of the record of their past lives. This personal humiliation was carried on further when they were informed at the hotel in Bucharest (a few days before their departure) that they would be charged the rate for foreigners, which is two and a half times that charged to natives, because they were no longer bona fide citizens of Romania.

Grandma Kern after having given David a bath in a
makeshift bathroom which doubles as a kitchen.

Itta Kern.   Itta and her son Isaac.

Abraham and Itta Kern in front of their mobile home in Israel, 1976.

David and Isaac Kern, Israel, 1976.

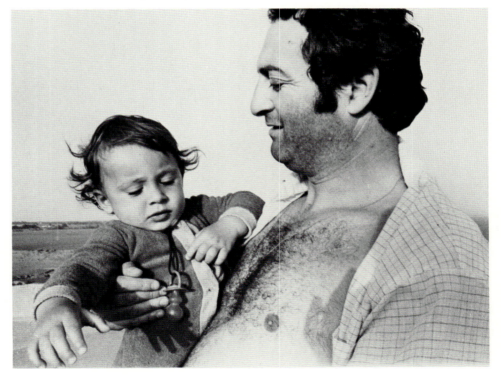

The Kerns' arrival in Israel was no release from restrictions. They were sent to an absorption center *(mercaz clita)*, where they were to learn the language and the Israeli way of life while waiting for suitable housing and jobs to turn up. Isaac had a very hard time finding a job that lived up to his aspirations. Israeli policy was to try to put the immigrants into new towns, but Isaac felt that these settlements would not have the kind of industry that could employ his skills. He and his family had to wait a year and a half, living in trailers, until he found a job in a place where he wanted to be.

There was a particularly sad twist to their experience in Israel.

When Abraham died a year after their arrival in Israel, Isaac was told that his father could not be buried in the community where they were living, because the cemetery had only enough space for those who had lived there for many years; Abraham would have to be buried far away. Isaac was able to reverse this decision, but it took a lot of talking to the proper authorities.

The Kamiels

Jacob Kamiel, as the *Kultos* president (president of the Jewish Committee) and a former history professor at the senior high school of Rădăuţi, commanded a great deal of respect from the Jewish as well as the non-Jewish population. He was very Germanic in his behavior: he used to say to Laurence, *"Laurenz, sei pünktlich, sei pünktlich"* (Laurence, be on time, be on time)—for Laurence had by then adopted the Romanian concept of time. In Jacob's spare time, when he was not at the Jewish Committee offices, he used to enjoy sitting in his comfortable living room to watch his favorite Romanian soccer team. Occasionally he would play backgammon or cards with his wife and her friends, and when Laurence would play with him, Mr. Kamiel would take delight in proving that he was a better player.

We were welcome guests at the Kamiels' home. Jacob's wife, Margit, used to make delicious desserts, such as chocolate cake with walnuts, and serve café au lait. We would frequently be invited to taste one of her specialties. Margit liked to gossip about other members of the Jewish community, and to offer her opinions on political and religious issues.

Professor Kamiel, as he liked to be called, was an ardent orator. His

Jacob Kamiel at home.

Rabbi Tirnauer officiating at the wedding of Danilla Kamiel to Raul Feldman under the traditional chuppa.

speeches were full of imperatives, guidelines for public behavior, and detailed descriptions of his negotiations with government officials and with Chief Rabbi Rosen, in Bucharest.

The Kamiels had an only daughter, Danilla. She chose to marry Raul Feldman, one of her colleagues, a fine Jewish man from Falticeni, a town nearby, where they both taught French at the local high school. Her wedding was the only one we attended during our two-year stay in Rădăuţi.

Danilla Kamiel's wedding reception was held at the Jewish Committee's offices, which were transformed for the occasion into a wedding hall. Mrs. Kamiel used her social connections to obtain the foods with which to prepare the feast for the reception. Laurence was even called upon to get

some scarce food items, such as walnuts from Bucharest. A local band was hired by the groom's family.

The wedding was very festive. The bride and groom went to Bucharest and Brasov for their honeymoon. One of the highlights of their trip was the flight to Bucharest—the very first flight for both of them.

What distinguished the older Kamiels from the rest of the community was that they had traveled in western Europe. Their daughter had the same formal education as the parents. She had chosen the right person to marry according to the parents; this left little room for family friction. Now their aspiration was to move to Israel together, and perhaps later to Germany, to continue their close-knit family life.

Kamiels and Feldmans four years after the wedding.

We received a postcard dated February 1, 1982, from the Kamiels, who now live in Israel. In a mixture of German, English, and Yiddish, they told us that they were learning Hebrew and were happy to be with their children, who were working and studying. The parents were looking forward to the possibility of working themselves after a certain period of adjustment, and were obviously in high spirits.

Jewish Baths

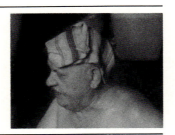

On Sunday mornings men carrying bunches of oak leaves were seen in the streets of the town. They walked in small groups headed in the direction of the Jewish baths on Strada Baia.

The baths, a vital part of the community life, were owned by the Jewish community and used by both the Jews and the Romanians. Laurence went there mainly to photograph things of Jewish interest, the mikva—a traditional religious bath—and the Jewish men and women working there.

Since the baths were about the only place where one could really get warm during the long, cold winter months, we both became frequent visitors to the steam bath and the hot showers. They were open Thursday, Friday, and Sunday; the morning hours would be reserved for women one day and for men the next. At any time, though, one could rent a private room with a tub. Friday was the busiest day, for it was the day of the market, and the day before the Jewish Sabbath. Peasants, before returning to their villages (after selling their goods at the market), would stop for a bath, and many members of the Jewish community would complete their Sabbath preparations there.

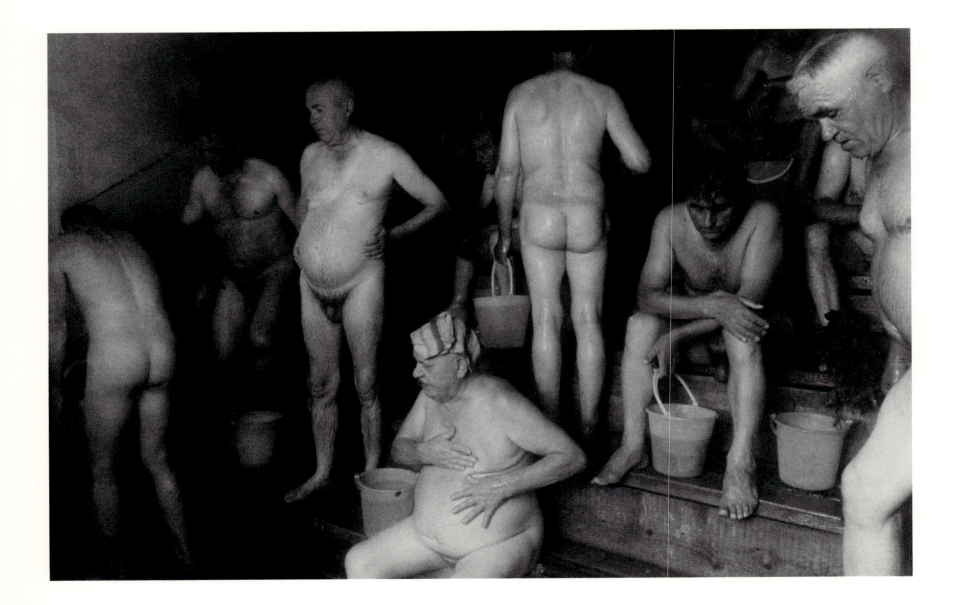

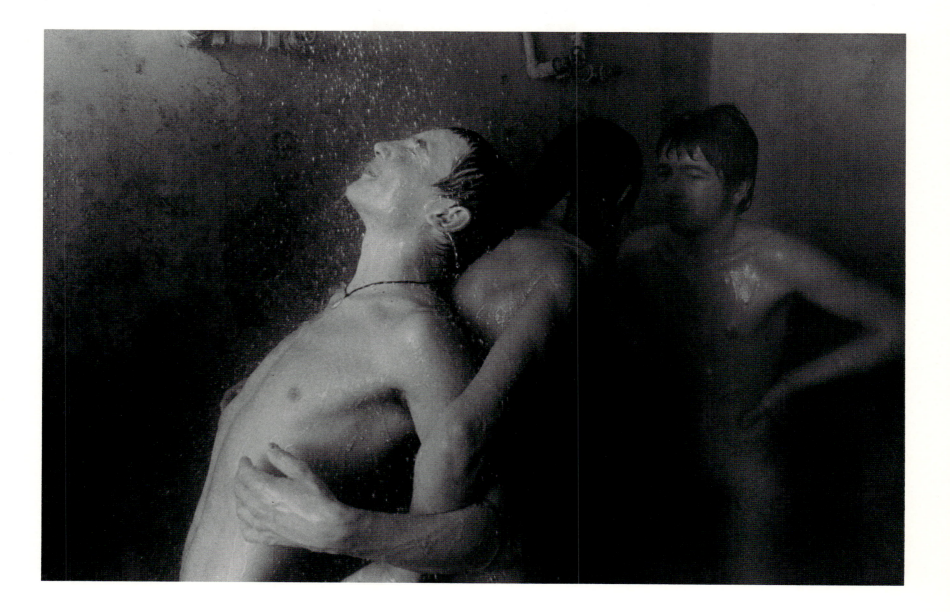

Sign on the door of the Jewish baths.

Mr. Moses Herskovitz, chief administrator of the baths.

The bathhouse was over a hundred years old. In a town where few of the houses had running water, it was a frequently visited place. Very little seemed to have changed since it was first built, except that the wooden buckets which were given out to each bather were replaced with plastic ones. The men filled their buckets with cold water as they walked into the steam room (abur). There were rows of wooden benches as in an amphitheater; the highest one was naturally the hottest.

The cold water in the bucket was used to refresh one's face and cool off a little as the steam began to get unbearable. A shrill bell rang several times, calling the bathers from other parts of the bathhouse to the steam

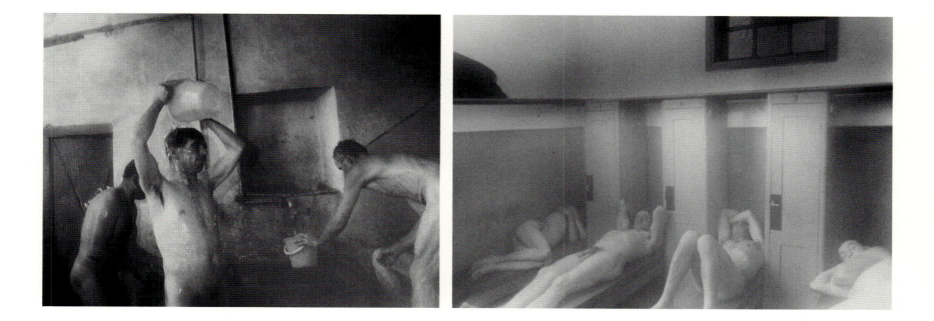

room. Often the room was so full that people were nearly sitting on top
of each other. The bath attendant opened the small iron door of the floor-
to-ceiling stove. Cups of cold water were thrown over the red hot stones
to let off more steam, and the men on the benches perspired more and
more. Waves of steam floated about. The hardy souls sitting on the upper
benches would shout "Heat up the bath! Heat up the bath!" (*Incalzeste
baia*). Then the whole process started again.

As the room began to cool down, men would beat each other's backs
with clusters of oak leaves that they had brought along with them. The
leaves stung the skin but left a wonderful, refreshing feeling and a sweet

smell. In the shower room there were always more people than shower heads. Sometimes a father and son would huddle together under one shower. After soaping up and bathing, the bathers would sometimes return for another session in the steam bath. The last station of the bath was the locker room, where totally relaxed, limp bathers lay down on the benches wrapped in coarse linen towels.

The bathing process was a ritual; the same men came week after week, joked around, and told stories to each other. It seemed that in the bath the problems of the outside world were washed away.

As one walked out of the bathhouse, near the locker room, one couldn't miss the following warning in bold type:

"Oamenii civilizati, nu scuipă pe jos, Deci serviţi-vă de scuipătoare!"

(Civilized people do not spit on the floor;
therefore, make use of the spitoon!)

Daily Bread

"There is no enterprise in the country which, even if it is exclusively Christian, does not have a Jew. In commercial and economic life they play the primary role. They possess much capital and have great properties." So wrote Father Dimitri Dan in his book on the Jews in the Bukovina region at the turn of the twentieth century. [*]

Prior to World War II there was a viable Jewish community of about 8,000 in Rădăuţi, which had a population of 22,000. The Jews were concentrated in one quarter, along Strada Putnei (see map, page 140), which led to the town's center. They and the Germans owned most of the stores and businesses. Only one fourth of the Jewish population survived the disasters of war and went back to Rădăuţi. Today the Jewish community comprises 220–240 people. In general, they lead the life of the Romanian middle class.

---

[*] "Die Juden in der Bukowina," in *Zeitschrift für Öster*, Wien, VI, 1890.

Harvesting of flax in the fall, in the fields near Rădăuţi.

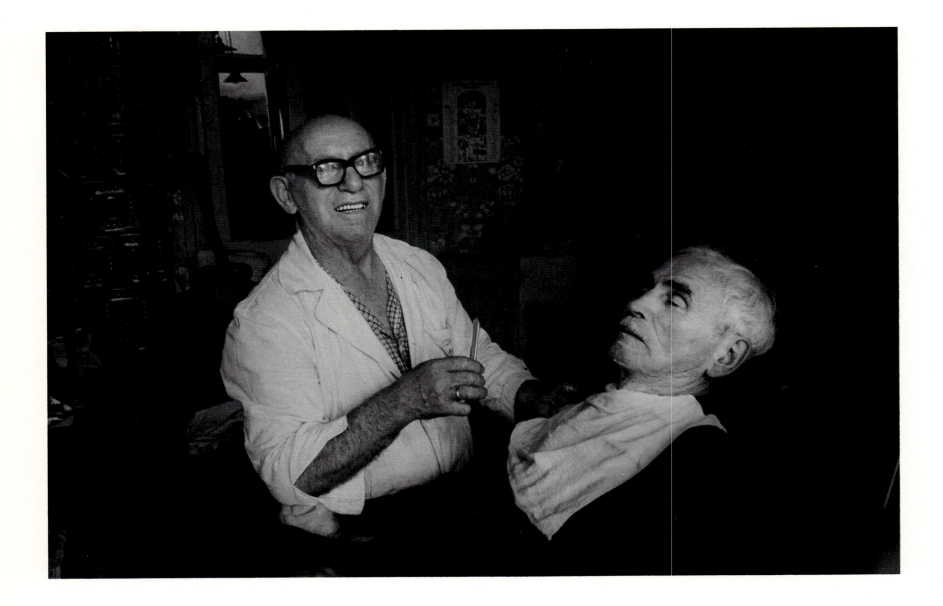

The Jewish Committee of Rădăuţi is *the* official organization. It conducts and manages the affairs of the Jewish community of Rădăuţi as well as some nearby communities that are now too small to have a committee of their own. Essentially, the Jewish Committee is the formal representative of the Jewish people to the Jewish Federation of Bucharest and the Romanian government. Known as the *Kultos Gemeinde* or *Comitatea Evreiasca,* the Jewish Committee evolved soon after the war to oversee and protect the needs and rights of the Jewish communities. The members of the committee meet daily to conduct their business: the management of the baths and the properties owned by the community, the maintenance of the synagogues and prayer houses and the Jewish cemeteries in the area. Then there is the sale of kosher meat and the distribution of supplementary food and clothing to the eligible poorer members of the community. These distributions are made four times a year and paid for by money sent from Bucharest, through JOINT, the International Jewish Organization. In 1975 JOINT gave the Jewish Federation of Romania three million dollars. Also, money from JOINT paid for the importation of various kosher foodstuffs from Israel for Passover, which, in turn, were sold to the Jewish community by the committee. Another crucial service provided by the committee is medical treatment and acquisition of drugs from abroad. On the cultural level, the committee, through the Jewish Federation of Bucharest, sponsors a performance by the Yiddish Jewish Theater of Bucharest once a year, a bimonthly newspaper (in Yiddish and Romanian), and a resident melamed (Hebrew teacher) for the young children.

Mr. Weisman, a barber in a nearby town. As a side job, he practices folk medicine, skillfully drawing blood with the help of his leeches.

At the time of our stay in Rădăuţi there were five administrative officers and seven to ten additional employees of the committee, presided over by Jacob Kamiel. President Kamiel was in his office daily from nine to three, looked over the daily agenda, made some phone calls, and dictated a few letters. The officers never seemed too occupied to chat or joke about each other's idiosyncrasies. However, Josef Gottlieb, the chief accountant, Mr. Weinstein, the bookkeeper, and Jacob Malik, the food supply attendant, were always very busy. Mr. Kamiel's duties were many and varied: in addition to overseeing the administration of the baths, he personally visited the old people, listened to their life histories, and many times persuaded them to sign over their homes or other property to the committee in return for a small pension. Thus more real estate was acquired and more cash generated from subsequent rentals.

Mr. Jacob Malik was the administrator of the food supply room. This was his second job—he was employed by the state as a *cojoc* maker (tailor of leather coats). Irwin Rosenbaum, the melamed, was a retired factory manager. He would travel to small towns in the vicinity of Rădăuţi and teach children Hebrew and the Torah.

Every Wednesday the Jews lined up inside the kosher butcher shop to buy meat for the week; if lucky, they would even get the cut they wanted. Meat was a dear item, so the Jews were privileged to have it every week.

Moses Lehrer framing "The Holy Birth" in his shop cluttered with glass and ancient tools.

Roza Wiener picked the feathers of freshly killed chickens every Thursday. She would separate the smaller ones for stuffing pillows.

The Jewish Committee paid salaries comparable to those paid by the state for similar services. It also offered attractive fringe benefits: employees could vacation at favorable spots, almost free, and had free admittance to the baths; they were usually able to acquire choice food or clothing without having to wait in distribution lines. Above all, they enjoyed the prestige of administering the community.

There were some complaints in Rădăuţi about injustices in the system. Mr. X, a retired craftsman, who had very little money to live on, was taken off the list of food recipients because "his son earns a lot of money—let him take care of his elderly parents." The fact of the matter was that Mr. X had not signed his house over to the committee and was not in a position to offer something in exchange for the committee's "act of favor." There was also a rumor that several years ago one of the present officers had embezzled a large amount of money from the community's coffers. Despite all the complaints, the majority of the people felt that the committee was an indispensable institution, rendering important services.

Among the officers of the committee Mr. Gottlieb and Mr. Wolitzer seemed most concerned about their self-importance. Mr. Gottlieb, the accountant, was fond of telling Laurence that he was by far the most important committee member, for, without his signature, none of the monies could be released. Mr. Wolitzer, the attorney, appeared to enjoy smoking foreign cigarettes; they were in fact local ones placed in a Benson and Hedges box that Laurence had given him. The humblest of all the men working for the committee was Mr. Baruch Weinstein. He was always bent over little bits of paper, trying to balance all the bills and debits. He was found of saying *"Herr Laurenz, so ist das"* (Mr. Laurence, so it is, nothing changes).

Moke Steiner made astrakhan hats in the cossack style. Each was carefully trimmed to fit on the wooden mold, which he kept in his attic workshop.

One of the large income-producing enterprises was the baths. All the proceeds from the baths went to the committee; the ticket taker, the towel holder, and the masseur all enjoyed free bathing as part of their employee benefits. Mr. Josef Gottlieb frequently boasted about having his private quarters in the bathhouse, where he went on Sunday mornings.

Most Jews, like most Romanians, worked at state-owned enterprises. Some people, however, were allowed to work independently. This group included self-employed artisans, farmers in marginally productive areas, and people working for religious organizations. The artisans, such as furriers, potters, tailors, and hat makers, were not permitted to supply raw materials—these had to be supplied by the clients. For instance, if one wanted to have a fur hat made, he had to bring a sufficient number of skins to the hat maker. The cost of labor was paid by the client, and the artisan or craftsman was expected to report his earnings to the government. Mr. Kern, the shoe repair man, Mr. Baruch, the mattress maker, Mrs. Weber, who made the Tyrolean-style hats for the peasants, and Moke Steiner, the fur hat maker were among those engaged in such private enterprises. Naturally, there was always the temptation to report less than the actual income earned. The usual practice was to negotiate a "good deal" for both the customer and the artisan that minimized the reportable income. Another characteristic of private dealings was bartering. Mrs. Weber, for instance, would often ask her customers to pay for their hats with dairy products, in addition to some cash.

Dr. Glatter, a self-taught dentist, grinding dentures in his kitchen.

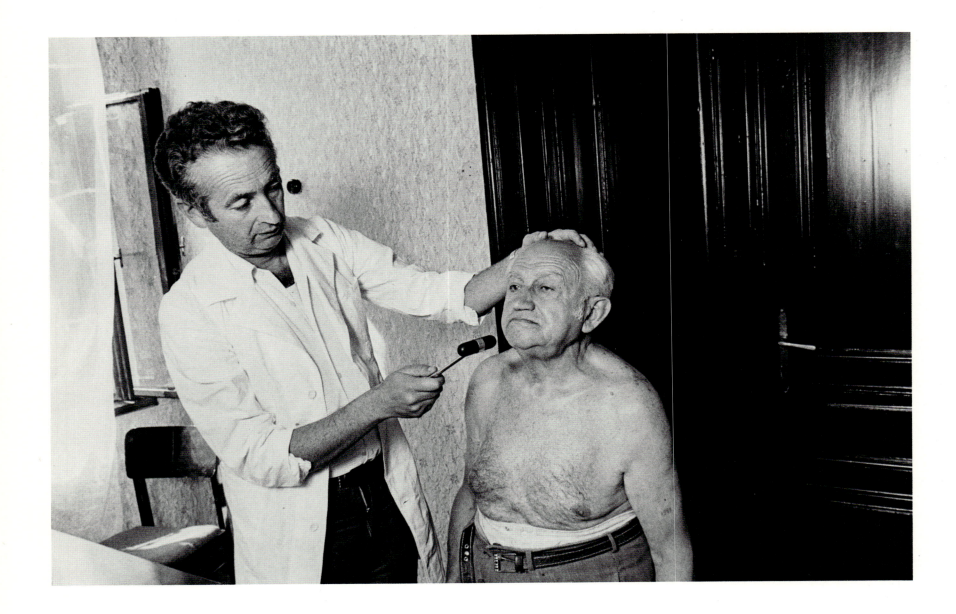

Most of the Jews of Rădăuţi who worked for the state supplemented their salary by moonlighting; some received a pension in addition to their salary. Frau Goldhirsch, for example, was retired and received a pension of four hundred lei from the state. She supplemented this income by running the candy concession at the movie theater. Her total monthly earnings amounted to fifty dollars. There were also Jewish doctors who combined private practice with employment at the state hospital.

Dr. Wolff gives Mr. Gottlieb his annual checkup at the local clinic.

Couples

The Dankners

When Samuel Dankner met Roza in the year 1914, he was a young lieutenant in the Austrian army and had just been called to the front. Before the outbreak of war he had been a student of law. Roza, together with her mother and four sisters, was fleeing the Russian armies that were occupying parts of the Bukovina region. Roza and Samuel kept in touch through letters, and in 1921 they were married. Between the wars Mr. Dankner worked in a bank in the part of Bukovina that is now within the boundaries of the U.S.S.R. He was also trained as an attorney, and when the Dankners went to Rădăuţi in 1945, Samuel practiced his profession there.

The Dankners invited us to their home and were eager to share their past life with us. They showed us some old photographs, including a wedding portrait, a picture of Samuel in his Austrian military uniform, and one of Roza in an elegant dress, silk stockings, pointed shoes, and a fashionable fur coat. This bundle of photographs, tied together with a piece of string, held fond memories. It was one of the few possessions that they were taking with them to Timisoara, a city in the southwest, where they planned to move to be with their son and his family. The young Dankner was a successful physician with a Ph.D. from the University of Timisoara.

Samuel and Roza Dankner.

The Dankners believed they could lead a good life in Romania, both as Jews and Romanian citizens. Samuel especially believed that the establishment of the Jewish Committee in 1948 was essential to ensure the organization of the Jewish community as a democratic entity along social and economic lines.

The Dankners and the Kamiels frequently visited each other, played card games, and arranged for other social events.

The Dankners invited us to their home in the afternoons; they always offered us freshly brewed coffee and delicious pastries that Samuel had bought from the pastry shop across the street from their house. We knew that both were dear items; but the Dankners' quiet, gracious manners created a mood in which we were able to enjoy their generous hospitality without feeling that we were imposing.

The Zweckers

Abraham and Helen Zwecker had been married for fifty-two years. Their faces and bodies were well weathered, but they held their heads up high and straight. Herr Zwecker, as he liked to be called, and Helen spoke German perfectly. They both had studied Greek and Latin at the university, and they quoted from the classical Greek poets and philosophers during the course of our conversations.

Helen missed her children and grandchildren who lived in Israel; tears would gather in her eyes when she looked at the color snapshots of them that she had placed in the mirror of her dresser. At such a moment Herr Zwecker would calm her with a lucid account of a happy event in the past. Then her frail body would stir from its slumped position, her hands clutching the lace handkerchief; within a few moments she would become lively, once again connected with the pleasant memories of the past.

They had lived in a big house with servants and two healthy children. He had worked hard and had become successful in the 1930s as the owner of the Solca beer factory, famous in Romania. He even gave us the secret recipe for making the beer. Back then, they were the aristocrats of Rădăuţi, well bred and well connected. In Herr Zwecker's words, "We were known

Abraham and Helen Zwecker in their living room. Another example of "riches to rags"—he was once the owner of the flourishing Solca brewery.

as big businessmen. Both Jews and Christians alike would greet us, acknowledge our presence, and ask us how we were. We were loved and esteemed."

Soon after their return from the labor camp in Transnistria, the beer factory and house were claimed by the socialist state. The house was rented out except for two of the rooms, where the Zweckers were allowed to live. Helen's Rosenthal china and Persian carpets had found their way into the homes of Communist party members in Bucharest, Oradea, and other cities. Most infuriating to them was that Herr Zwecker was given the job of selling tobacco, newspapers, and postcards in a cardboard kiosk. (Ironically, the kiosk was situated across the street from the large restaurant-hotel complex that his family had once owned.) But, Herr Zwecker told us, he was still able to sustain his sanity and dignity because of his motto: Whatever you do, do well and think of the end.

Helen Zwecker died of a heart attack in 1976. When I heard of her death, Abraham Zwecker's words about his wife echoed through my mind: "Nothing is more lofty or beautiful than my wife."

Herr Zwecker had a graceful way about him.

The Lehrers

Mr. and Mrs. Lehrer worked in a state-owned framing shop. Laurence first met Moses Lehrer in the synagogue. He was a cohen and led the services in the Wiznitzer Shul in the absence of the rabbi. His life was devoted to maintaining the synagogue, and he would often use his days off to repair its old windows and doors.

He was also the busiest person in town on Saturday nights. After prayers, the rabbi, the president of the community, and all the old and poor men would sit at long tables socializing, while Mr. Lehrer distributed the humble meal: challa, sardines, apples, and soft drinks. After dinner he would cut the cake baked by his wife. He always stretched the meal so that everyone got a little bit. Then he would smile with satisfaction until the tip of his nose nearly touched his fleshy upper lip. Moses Lehrer took his religious duties very seriously, and his wife likewise supported all the synagogue activities. She not only planted the small garden in the back of their house with tomatoes, onions, and cucumbers but also grew vegetables and flowers in the garden of the synagogue, all in preparation for Succoth.

Zile, as Mrs. Lehrer liked to be called, welcomed friends to drop by their shop on the way to the open market. The Lehrers knew the whole community and were well liked and respected; it seemed that except for

Zile and Moses Lehrer. They devoted their lives to the maintenance of the Wiznitzer Shul and the garden behind it.

their son's absence, living in Rădăuţi was completely satisfactory for the Lehrers. But they were still deciding whether or not to depart for Israel, where Moses' sisters had gone about twenty-five years before, or for western Europe to join their son, who had been gone about two years.

The Steiners

Moke and Hortensia Steiner are a unique couple; she is a peasant woman of Romanian Orthodox background whom Moke, a Jewish city dweller, met during his fur and sheep trading transactions with Hortensia's parents and their neighbors. Her family still lives in a small village, not far from Rădăuţi.

Moke was paralyzed on his right side toward the end of World War II. A German soldier shot him in the head while he was escaping out of a window of a house in which there were sixty young boys. The Germans set the house on fire and Moke was the only survivor. It was a miracle that he survived.

As Moke was talking, Hortensia was preparing a fabulous lunch for us. She was a big woman, with full cheeks that obscured her twinkling eyes when she smiled. Although she was about fifteen years younger than Moke, she doted on him as she did upon their thirteen-year-old son. "Moke, you must take a rest this afternoon. I'll prepare the fur for the hats. Moke, don't talk too loud—neighbors will hear you and then we may get into trouble." And so on.

Moke and his wife were living in a state of anxiety. They were afraid that the police would discover that they owned some astrakhan fur, which they made into hats and sold privately. The state owned all livestock and its by-products (except for the small number of sheep owned individually for subsistence). But the Steiners occasionally took chances, and were very careful in choosing their clients.

Hortensia would often joke about Moke's "hidden gold" and the absurdities of being hassled by the police; once she and Moke put on a short morality skit for just the two of us, in their kitchen, in which they were portrayed as villains being sought out by the benevolent state. As the iron hand of the state pressed down on their heads, they sank down, pleading. (Before the skit was put on, the son was discreetly sent outside to play with his friends.) This skit afforded comic relief, a means of coping with the absurdities of the state laws.

The Steiners had a successful working relationship. While Moke went to the marketplace to solicit customers for hats, Hortensia would be sewing the stretched skins into hats and placing them on molds. Although Moke was an invalid, he carried himself very well, without showing much concern for his short leg and his small, shriveled right hand. When he limped along to the marketplace he held himself very straight. He always appeared to be very certain about his specific task of approaching the right people at the marketplace, and persuading them to go to his house to buy his hats. He was an expert salesman, tenacious and soft-spoken. In his attic workshop, the same one his father had used, he would pick up a hat with his left hand made into a fist, and start turning it around with his thumb, examining Hortensia's stitches.

To show her allegiance to Moke, Hortensia had converted to Judaism and even spoke some Yiddish. Although they chose to remain outside the small Jewish social circle, they celebrated all the holidays. Moke attended services regularly and Hortensia cooked many of the traditional Jewish foods.

After we returned to the United States, we learned that the Steiners had left for Israel in the spring of 1977. They were placed in an apartment

Moke and Hortensia Steiner—a Jewish furrier married to a Romanian farm girl who converted to Judaism.

Kivi Steiner holding up his passport as the Steiners prepare to depart for Israel.

for immigrants at Yok'nam. Hortensia is now working in a cookie factory, packing boxes during the night shift. She is very determined to make the best of it. While she is investigating the possibility of starting a fur business in Israel or in the United States their son Kivi is attending high school and Moke is temporarily employed as a guard. Being an invalid, Moke can find little work. He is very discouraged in Israel; he feels foreign to the automated society in which he is now living and would have to be trained to fit into a new mold. He can no longer come and go as he wishes, the way he did in the marketplace of Rădăuţi. There he was somebody—he fulfilled a certain demand. In Yok'nam he is just another immigrant, and unskilled at that. His sense of dignity is shattered. Although he has gone back to Rădăuţi several times, he was not able to remain there either.

In Israel, we found him sitting in the kitchen all day, surrounded by modern kitchen wares, his head between his hands, muttering in German *"Verstehen Sie, Laurenz?"* (Do you understand, Laurence?) Of course, we could never understand all that he wanted to say.

Aging

We met only a handful of old people who lived alone. They were usually people who had outlived all their immediate relatives. The anguish of being alone was clearly visible on their faces. One such person was Frau Dr. Rath, née Weiss, of Storojinets. Frau Rath's lawyer husband had been dead for many years, and her son, a veterinarian, lives in Lima, Peru. She was born in 1883 and was now the last surviving Jew of the town of Solca, a small town twenty kilometers from Rădăuţi. Before the war Solca had a community of about four hundred Jewish people. Frau Dr. Rath was looked after by a Romanian family in whose house she was a tenant. On several occasions Laurence visited her with Jacob Kamiel, who as the head of the Jewish community was responsible for looking after the needs of people such as Frau Dr. Rath. (Jacob Kamiel was also the supervisor of the caretaker of the Jewish cemetery in Solca.)

Frau Dr. Rath, on one occasion, said to Laurence, "*Allein so lebe ich Tag und Nacht, allein das sind die schwersten Momente*" (Alone as I live day and night, alone these are the most difficult moments). Jacob Kamiel cared very deeply about her. He wanted to make sure that she was eligible to receive a pension, food, and clothing from the Jewish Federation of Bucharest. Unless the old people were asked to sign their wills, they would never get around to doing so, and consequently the Romanian state would

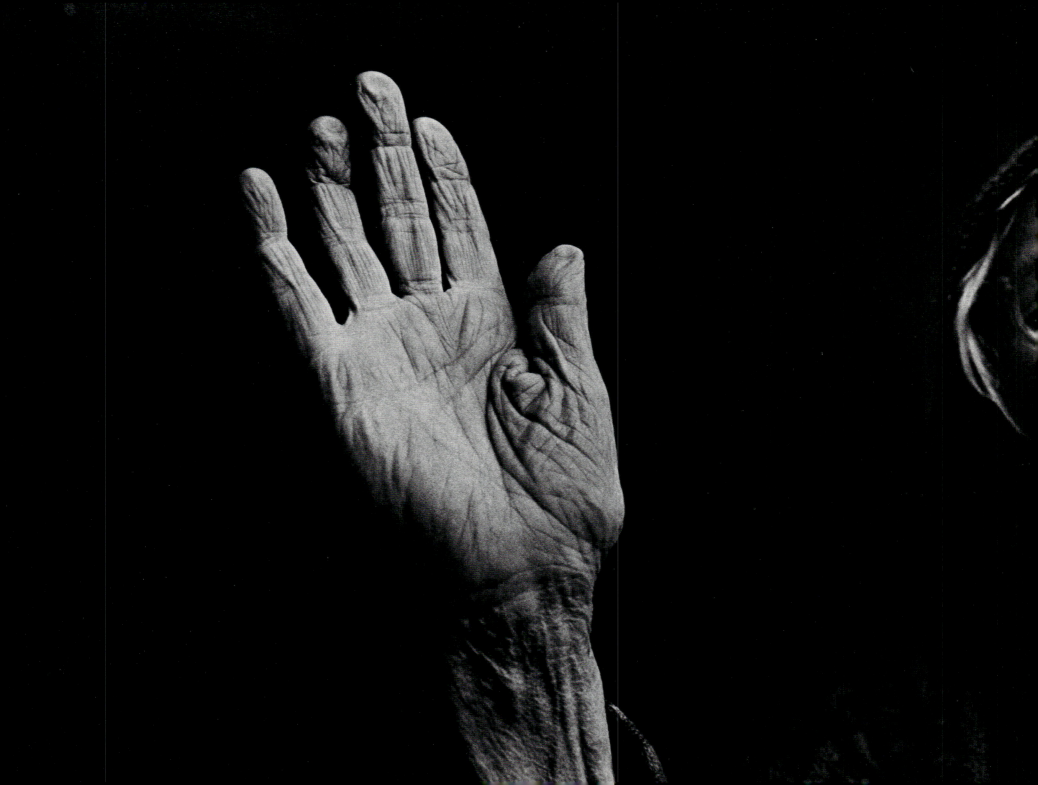

Frau Rath, the only Jewish person left in Solca, a town near Rădăuţi.

Frau Rath signs her will, giving her belongings to the Jewish Committee.

The rabbi cutting off a piece from Nathan Thau's lapel. The act symbolizes the breaking of the link between Thau and his father.

inherit the wealth of the Jewish community. After Jacob Kamiel explained the benefits to her, Frau Dr. Rath was ready to sign her will. She had few belongings. It was more important to her to receive a pension and the additional food supplement than it was to keep her belongings to herself. She did not even have a distant relative who could inherit them.

The Jews of Rădăuţi were old, but they had created support systems to keep them and their community going. In western societies, where people are linked to one another by circumstance rather than by choice and where family ties do not extend beyond the nuclear family, old age is equated with aloneness. Help from family is frequently replaced by institutional care. The old-age home is purely a western phenomenon. It provides basic comforts of life, health care, and some companionship, but it prevents the elderly from participating in the lives of their close kin.

The Jewish community in Rădăuţi is largely made up of people in their late fifties and older. As young people, these men and women had experienced much deprivation, bad health, and the loss of most of their close relatives in concentration camps. Yet they had survived. They had come back to Rădăuţi from camps in Transnistria in the late 1940s because they needed to come back "home." It represented the only familiarity to them, even though they found destruction where their homes had been. From then on they concentrated their energies on working hard, knitting close ties with their kin, and providing a good future for their children. Now, as old people, they are sickly and infirm, but they live in their memories of the past. Their hopes are built upon the successful endeavors of their children.

During our two years in Rădăuţi we went to about fifteen funerals. In the beginning we did not know the person whose funeral we were attending, but before long we were attending the funerals of people whom Laurence had photographed.

The news of a death, Jewish or Christian, spread very quickly throughout

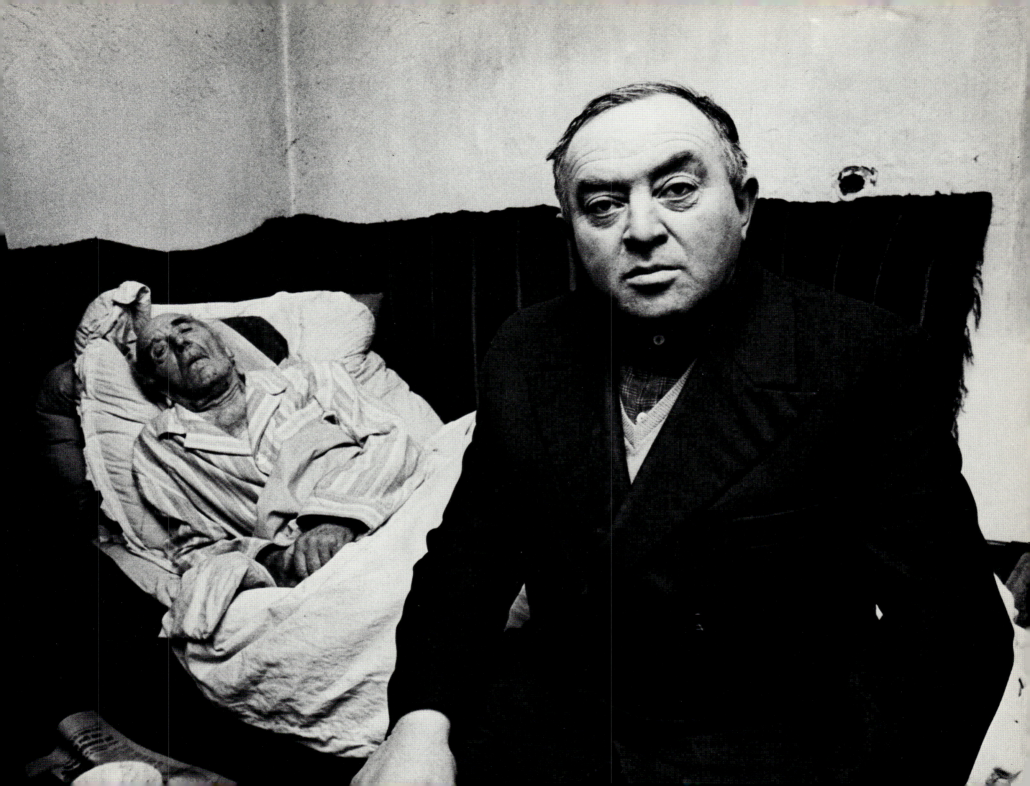

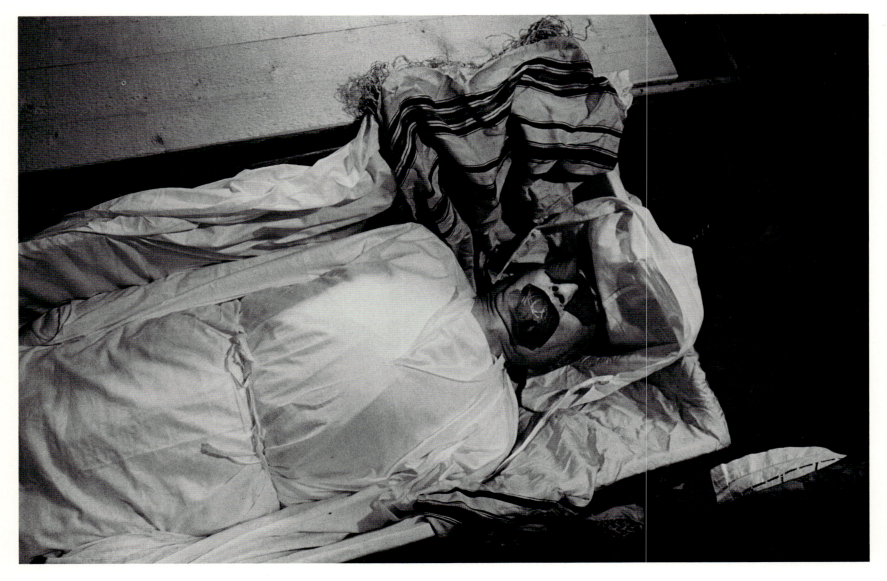

Black potsherds covering eyes and mouth.

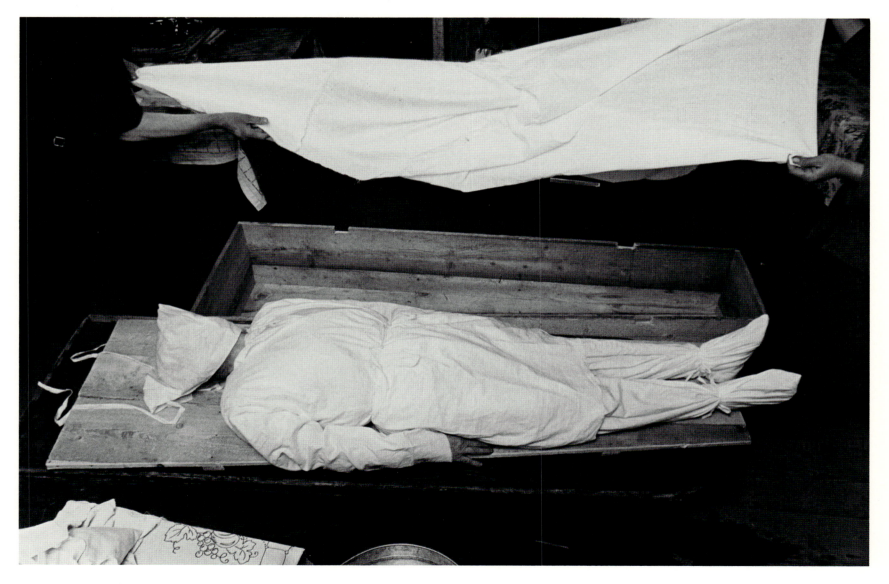

Mr. Leizer Cohen's body prepared for his funeral.

the town. The Jewish Committee's offices would be full of activity and lively discussions of plans for the funeral. First Bubbi Leizer had to be notified to get the horse-drawn hearse, which was kept behind the Jewish baths. Then the ritual washers had to be called in. Also the Romanian peasant woman who looked after the cemetery had to be told to dig the grave. A death certificate had to be filled out, the rabbi had to be called in, and a bus chartered to carry the mourners to the cemetery. The committee officers took these duties very seriously.

Josef Levy would usually be among the first to arrive at the house of the deceased, for he was one of the ritual washers. According to tradition, the body is washed in vinegar, then a raw egg is broken and thrown into the pan which contains the washed-off vinegar. The body is then dressed in a white, baglike suit, called *tachrichim*, which is sewn for the occasion. Finally, when the body is placed in a simple, pine coffin, a black ceramic jug is smashed on the floor and the larger pieces are used to cover the eyes and the mouth of the deceased.

At one funeral Laurence overheard a dispute between Josef Levy and the family members of the deceased. Josef Levy said, "You are lucky. If there were two of us here, you would have to pay double the price!" In Rădăuți the ritual washer was paid about fifteen dollars for his services, and the total cost of the funeral, including the digging of the grave, was less than a hundred dollars.

After the washing of the body the mourners would already be in the front room of the house or waiting in the courtyard outside. The closed coffin was set out in the room on two low stools. The rabbi entered, gave a short service, and symbolically tore part of the clothing of the closest relative of the deceased. Then the coffin was draped with a black flag with the Star of David on it, and carried out to the waiting horse-drawn hearse.

It was incredible that we would even be allowed to be present in the

Marcus Lefkowitz—in his youth he had fought the Germans, as a member of a Russian partisan group. Here, he is making the sign of the cohen.

room where the preparation of the body took place. I had never seen as bitter an expression of grief on anyone's face as I saw on Mrs. Postelnik's when the last nail was hammered into the lid of her brother's coffin, sealing it tightly. She lifted up her arms in disbelief, clenching her hands tightly over her head in a gesture of nonacceptance. Where was he going?

The funeral procession started with the closest members of the family following behind the hearse. Passing through the main streets of Rădăuţi, the procession of men and women stopped in front of the synagogue, where the men prayed and said kaddish. A chartered bus followed close behind the heels of the mourners. One by one, the people got on the bus, so that by the time the procession reached the cemetery, there were only one or two people left following the coffin on foot.

Laurence remembers one cold winter day when the bus had not been chartered, because of some misunderstanding, and the mourners had to

walk the full distance. He said he thought there would be one or two more deaths that day—among the mourners. Many of them were old and seemed too feeble to take such a long walk.

At the cemetery, the coffin was carried into a small chapel where the rabbi eulogized the deceased. Later, as the coffin was lowered into the grave, each person there took a handful of earth and threw it in. Toward the end of the funeral ceremony many people would take the time to visit the graves of their close relatives, light candles, and whisper short prayers. Then, as the mourners departed from the cemetery, they stopped at the gate to wash their hands.

There are still plenty of empty spaces in the Jewish cemetery of Rădăuţi. Some enterprising peasants have already planted potatoes in the last few empty rows. They will probably continue to harvest this land long after the last Jewish person in Rădăuţi is dead.

The centuries-old
Jewish cemetery of Rădăuţi.

Afterword: *Return to Rădăuți*

Laurence Salzmann

In September of 1979 I returned to Rădăuți to continue the documentation of the *Last Jews of Rădăuți* project. This was my first visit back to Rădăuți in three years. An editor from GEO magazine had seen the photographic exhibit at the International Center of Photography in New York City, and he called me to do an article for the magazine. I returned to Rădăuți with the writer, Dan Rottenberg, to take more photographs and document changes that had taken place within three years.

I suggested going there in September because it coincided with the Jewish High Holy Days. In Rădăuți, as in most Jewish communities, this is a time when people get together. Also, September is a beautiful month in Rădăuți: the summer's harvest is ripe and many fruits and vegetables are available, including a delicious wild strawberry which is found nowhere else except in the mountain valley surrounding the town. I was anxious to return to Rădăuți to find answers to questions, such as who was still alive, who had moved away, what were the feelings of those still remaining about emigrating to Israel. Also, I wanted to explore another dimension— the youth.[*] Were they continuing the traditions of their fathers? What were their parents' hopes and plans for their children?

[*] That aspect of my study which involved the Jewish youth was funded by the Memorial Foundation for Jewish Culture. I would like to thank them for their support.

130

As soon as I arrived in Bucharest, the first item on my agenda was to visit with Rabbi Rosen, the chief rabbi of Romania, in order to secure his permission to go back to Rădăuţi. I also wanted to present him with a set of original prints from my *Last Jews of Rădăuţi* series for the new Jewish History Museum in Bucharest. I had heard that the rabbi had not been too pleased with the title of my show. In a speech at Chanuka time, last year, he had said that it was not yet time to say kaddish for the Jews of Rădăuţi. I decided to leave out the box which had the title printed on the cover and just give him the photographs. "Why don't you photograph our young choir here in Bucharest?" asked the rabbi. "Why always these old *babas*?" I told him that this time I was going to concentrate on the youth. The rabbi thanked me for my gift. Though he didn't always agree with my point of view, he did concede that the Jewish community of Romania was no longer a flourishing one! Then he called the Jewish Committee office in Rădăuţi on my behalf to tell them of my arrival.

Had Rădăuţi changed? Alighting from the train I discovered that there were no more taxis. One of the things the state had done to save energy was to eliminate taxis in small towns and to cut out the use of streetlights at night. Many of the cobblestone streets had been paved over, but the center of the town was still intact.

I had been informed earlier that many of the people I had known were no longer living in Rădăuţi. They were dead or had gone to Israel. Among the most missed was the rabbi, Josef Tirnauer. I was interested in knowing who had replaced him and how the people felt about their loss. A shochet (ritual butcher) had replaced him; he was on a two-year contract from Israel. He did not command the respect that Rabbi Tirnauer had. I met him, unfortunately, on an occasion when a Jewish woman was scolding him for keeping the women with their chickens waiting outside while he was giving advice to some Romanian peasants who had come to see him. It was an embarrassing situation, to say the least.

Mr. Lehrer in his succah—he is following the tradition of his forefathers in building a succah each year.

Laurence presenting Rabbi Rosen, the chief rabbi of Romania, with a set of his photographs.

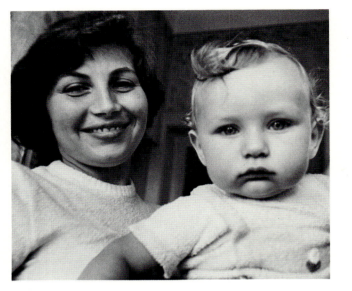

Henie and son. "I think we will all be in Israel next year," she said. She was a practicing pediatrician who had decided to dedicate herself to living and working in Israel.

Services were no longer conducted by members of the congregation. There were still three prayer houses open for Sabbath services. They barely managed to get a minyan for each service, and they would often trade members to complete the minyan in order to commence the services. More than half of the members of the Wiznitzer Shul, which was still maintained by Moses Lehrer, had died or emigrated. Moses and his wife were still trying to decide whether they should join members of their family residing in Israel, or be with their son in western Europe.

Rabbi Brael Bronfman, the new shochet for Rădăuţi and environs, came from Israel on a two-year contract to replace Rabbi Tirnauer.

Beatrice Weinstein with her mother and grandmother. She is a graduate of the mathematics faculty at the University of Iasi. Her plans are to stay in Romania.

I noticed that the older people didn't feel they were being pushed out by the state, but pulled by their children who had already left and were urging them to leave. Almost everyone had a relative in Israel, Germany, or the United States. The parents' ambivalence about leaving was well founded: after a certain age how easily could they adapt to a new social setting?

There are about twenty-three young Jewish people (from infants to people in their thirties) left in Rădăuţi. They either live with their parents

Misu Baruch before his departure for Israel. He wanted to explore his opportunities there since his prospects in Rădăuţi were limited.

or have families of their own. Almost all share the common desire to leave Romania. Most of them are planning to settle in Israel, a few will go to Germany. They want to leave basically because they do not feel that they are a part of the Romanian nation and want to go somewhere with a larger Jewish community of which they can be a part. They also want to live where opportunities for employment are better. The only question is when they will move. Some are waiting for their parents to reach the eligibility age for a pension in Israel. Older people are waiting for their children to be finished with their schooling. To leave or to stay is not always an easy question to resolve. One young person told me that she thought of her generation as a sacrificed generation, that they did not really fit into

Romanian or Israeli life-styles. Many, in anticipation of departure, make a preliminary visit to Israel, ostensibly to see relatives, but actually to observe what life is like there, should they decide to emigrate. One young man I knew in Rădăuţi returned after having gone to Israel. He said he missed home and did not care for the Israeli way of life.

Almost everybody I knew was at the synagogue during High Holy Days—Rosh Hashanah services were attended by a big crowd. Hermy Buchsenspanner, a five-year-old with a devilish grin, ate a cookie as he sat with his grandmother. Feeling a little bored, he came and sat down next to me. He asked endless questions. His father had not come with him to services, because he had to go to his job at a state-owned farm. Young people like Hermy's father usually did not sit through the whole service. Most put in an appearance, which seemed to say "I am one of you, but I cannot follow the service with the same devotion as you elderly folks do." At the end of services everyone came up to wish me a happy New Year. For me it was like going home, because I knew the whole congregation. Once again I began to receive invitations to visit with people in their homes. They were interested in learning about Ayşe and our daughter Han, and in seeing their pictures. They knocked on wood and wished them good health and many happy years.

Hermy Buchsenspanner.

Ayşe Salzmann

In August 1982, with our three-and-a-half-year-old daughter, we returned to Rădăuţi for a very brief visit, to see the people we knew and to see the wonderful Friday market once again. The concierge at the hotel was the man who used to be the assistant manager. Now he ran the hotel. He gave us our old room, number 12, overlooking the main intersection of the town.

What were the changes in the Jewish community? We knew that Rabbi Tirnauer had died, and Professor Kamiel had left for Israel with his family. So the community had lost two of its leaders. We found out that with deaths and emigration the Jewish population has been diminished by a half. Those who remain are mostly confined to their homes, their thoughts oriented to their children living abroad. The Jewish Committee is still functioning, but its services are at a minimum. Its capital base of 600,000 lei is guarded carefully; yet people who are in dire need of aid are denied it. The only occasions for social contact among the people of the community are the services at the synagogue and at the funerals. "In five years time there will not be a Jewish community in Rădăuţi," said one of our friends.

The older people I talked to seemed to feel that they would not be willing to leave for Israel. A visit for a few weeks was all right, but their children might find a permanent stay burdensome, they thought. Some of their contemporaries who had emigrated had died shortly after their arrival—perhaps the shock of a new culture and a new climate had been too great.

We heard a joke about Jewish emigration told by a Romanian in Rădăuţi: "Srul is going from Romania to Israel by boat; Isac is on another boat coming from Israel. Somewhere on the open sea their boats pass. The two men wave to each other. Srul says to Isac, 'Where are you going, you unlucky one?' Isac, characteristically, answers the question with another question, 'Where are *you* going, you unlucky one?' "

One day, by a stroke of luck, we met Isaac Kern and his family in front of the hotel. They had come back from Israel for a month's visit to Romania. Isaac had brought his children to show them where their grandfather had lived, worked and prayed. He and Laurence attended services at the synagogue, and they went to the baths together.

The Kerns were doing well in Israel; the children looked healthy and they spoke Hebrew and Romanian. But Isaac missed the quality of human relationships, the close ties between friends and family members, that he had experienced in Romania. His wife, Leah, on the other hand, was unequivocally happy in Israel. After her mother's death, her last tie with Romania had been ruptured. Isaac kept on saying, "If only there was more liberty in Romania. . . ." Would he then really have stayed?

A few days later we exchanged good-byes with Isaac and Leah, again in front of the hotel, promising to meet in Philadelphia or in Tel Aviv. Such promises would have been pipe dreams for the Kerns seven years ago. Now they can move freely, to their hearts' content.

The Jewish community of Rădăuţi is like an old tapestry: it is threadbare and the designs have faded; as the old die and the young leave, the interlocking threads come loose.

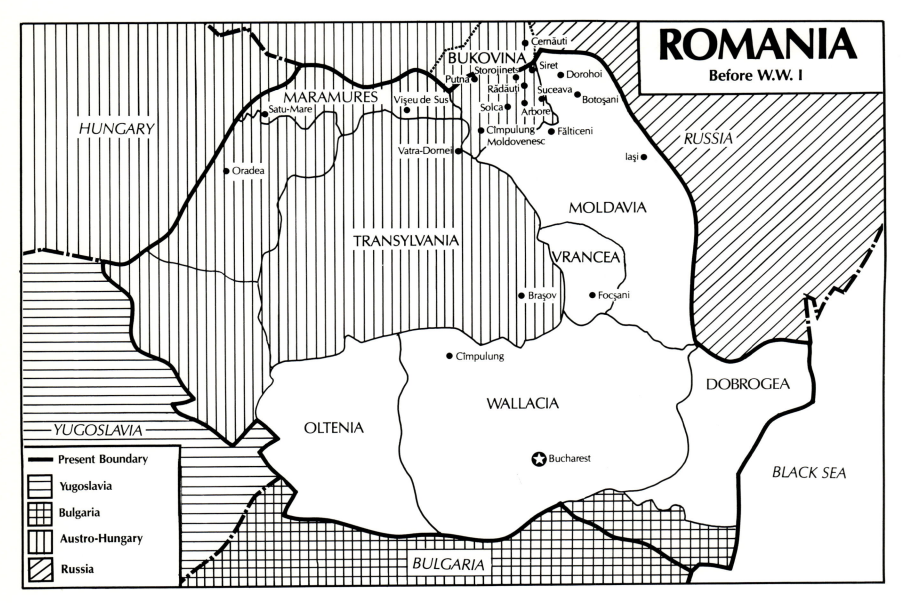

ROMANIA
Before W.W. I

HUNGARY

MARAMURES

Satu-Mare

Oradea

Viṣeu de Sus

BUKOVINA

Cernăuţi

Putna Storojineţs Siret Dorohoi

Rădăuţi Suceava

Solca Arbore Botoşani

Cîmpulung Fălticeni
Moldovenesc

Vatra-Dornei

RUSSIA

Iaşi

MOLDAVIA

TRANSYLVANIA

VRANCEA

Braşov Focşani

Cîmpulung

DOBROGEA

WALLACIA

OLTENIA

YUGOSLAVIA

⭐ Bucharest

BLACK SEA

Present Boundary

Yugoslavia

Bulgaria

Austro-Hungary

Russia

BULGARIA

138

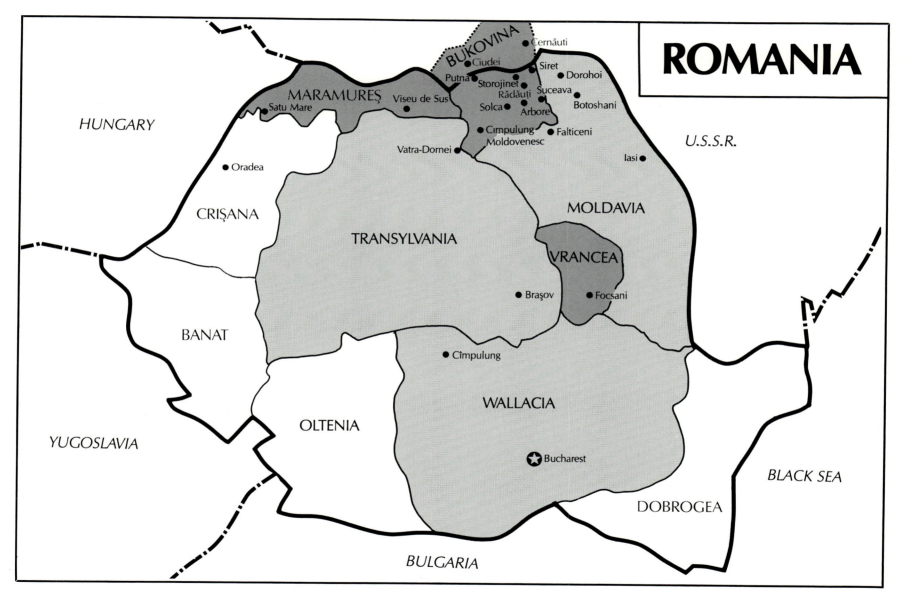

ROMANIA

HUNGARY

BUKOVINA

Cernăuti
Ciudei
Putna
Siret
Storojinet
Dorohoi
Rădăuți
Suceava
Solca
Arbore
Botoshani
Cimpulung
Falticeni
Moldovenesc
Vatra-Dornei
Iasi

MARAMUREŞ
Viseu de Sus
Satu Mare

U.S.S.R.

Oradea

CRIŞANA

MOLDAVIA

TRANSYLVANIA

VRANCEA

BANAT

Braşov
Focsani

Cîmpulung

YUGOSLAVIA

OLTENIA

WALLACIA

★ Bucharest

BLACK SEA

DOBROGEA

BULGARIA

139

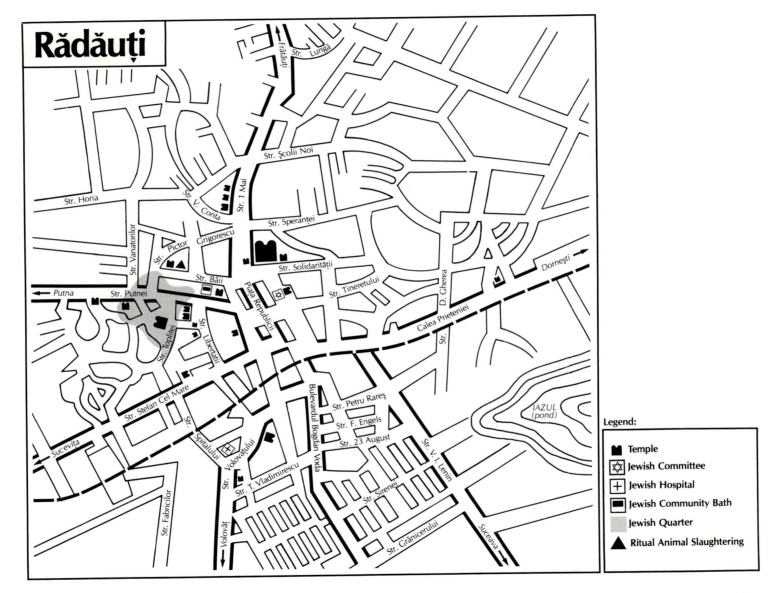

Rădăuți

Str. Frătăuți
Str. Lungă
Str. Şcolii Noi
Str. 1 Mai
Str. Horia
Str. V. Conta
Str. Speranţei
Str. Vanatorilor
Str. Pictor Grigorescu
Str. Solidarităţii
Str. Băii
← Putna
Str. Putnei
Piaţa Republicii
Str. Tineretului
D. Gherea
Dorneşti →
Str. Topliţei
Str. Libertăţii
Calea Prieteniei
Str.
Str. Ştefan Cel Mare
Sucevita
Str. Fabricilor
Str. Spitalului
Str. Volovatului
Volovăţ →
Str. T. Vladimirescu
Bulevardul Bogdan Voda
Str. Petru Rareş
Str. F. Engels
Str. 23 August
Str. Sirenei
Str. V. I. Lenin
Str. Grănicerului
Suceava
IAZUL (pond)

Legend:

- Temple
- Jewish Committee
- Jewish Hospital
- Jewish Community Bath
- Jewish Quarter
- Ritual Animal Slaughtering

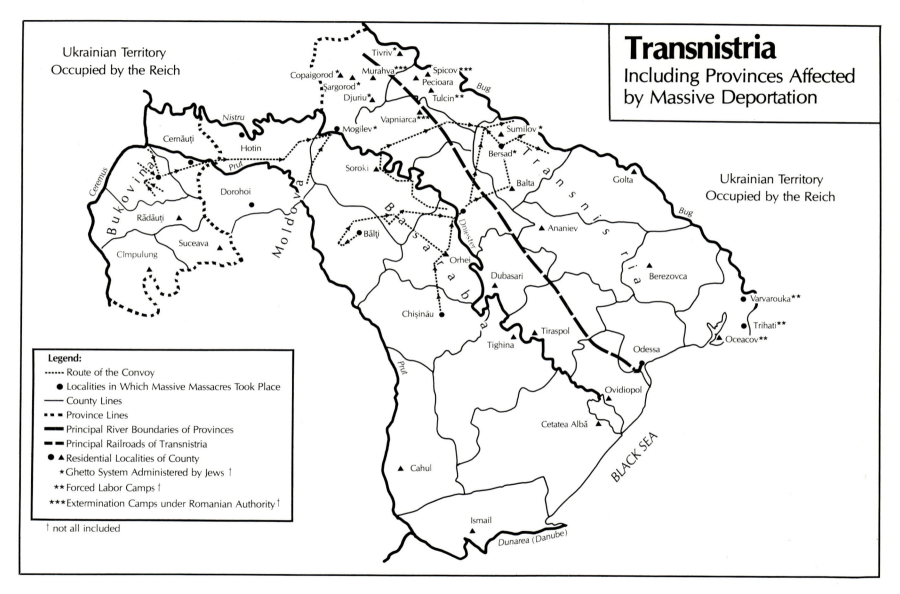

Transnistria
Including Provinces Affected by Massive Deportation

Ukrainian Territory Occupied by the Reich

Ukrainian Territory Occupied by the Reich

Tivriv *▲
Copaigorod *▲   Murahva *** ▲   Spicov *** ▲
Şargorod *   ▲ Pecioara
Djuriu *▲   Tulcin **
Vapniarca ***
Mogilev *   ▲ Sumilov *
Bersad *
Balta ▲   Golta
Soroki ▲
Bălţi ●   ▲ Ananiev
Orhei   ▲ Berezovca
Dubasari ▲
Chişinău ●   Varvarouka **
Tiraspol ▲   Trihati **
Tighina ▲   ▲ Oceacov **
                 Odessa
Ovidiopol ▲
Cetatea Albă ▲
Cahul ▲
Ismail ▲
Dunarea (Danube)
BLACK SEA

Cernăuţi
Hotin ●
Dorohoi ●
Rădăuţi ▲
Suceava ▲
Cîmpulung

Nistru
Prut
Ceremuş
Bukovina
Moldova
Basarabia
Dniester
Bug
Transnistria

Legend:
------ Route of the Convoy
● Localities in Which Massive Massacres Took Place
—— County Lines
▬▬▬ Province Lines
━━━ Principal River Boundaries of Provinces
━ ━ ━ Principal Railroads of Transnistria
● ▲ Residential Localities of County
  * Ghetto System Administered by Jews †
 ** Forced Labor Camps †
*** Extermination Camps under Romanian Authority †

† not all included

141

Glossary

Bar Mitzva   A ceremony to formally admit as an adult member of the Jewish community a boy thirteen years old. Also refers to the boy himself.

brith   The celebration at the Brith Milah.

Brith Milah   The rite of circumcision of Jewish male children.

challa   White bread served at Sabbath or festival meals.

Chanuka   Feast of Dedication or Feast of Lights, celebrating rededication of Temple in 167 B.C.E.

Chasid   A follower of a movement in Jewish orthodoxy characterized by emphasis on prayer, mysticism, and joy in worship.

cohen   A Jew of priestly descent.

gabbai   Officer of a synagogue.

kaddish   Prayer recited in memory of a departed relative.

Kiddush   Benediction for sanctification of Sabbath and holiday, recited over wine.

kosher   Ritually acceptable in accordance with Jewish religious practice and dietary laws.

melamed   A Hebrew teacher, usually elementary.

mikva   Ritual bath of purification prepared according to prescribed regulations.

minyan   A quorum; ten men above the age of thirteen required for public worship.

mohel (moyel)   One who performs the rite of circumcision.

Rosh Hashanah   Jewish New Year, occurring on the first day of the month of Tishri (in the fall).

shul   A Jewish place of worship; a synagogue.

Shabbes   The Sabbath, day of rest on seventh day of the week; prescribed by one of the Ten Commandments.

Shabbes goy   A non-Jew employed to perform various acts of work prohibited to Jews on the Sabbath.

shnaps   Liquor.

shochet   One who slaughters animals or fowls according to Jewish ritual.

Succoth   Feast of Tabernacles, occurring on fifteenth day of Tishri.

tachrichim   Shroud of white linen in which the dead are arrayed for burial.

tefillin   Phylacteries; inscription on parchment encased in two small leather cubicles. They are placed on forehead and left arm when praying.

Wiznitzer Chasid   A Chasid from the town of Wiznitz.

Yiddish   Language spoken by Jews since around 1000 C.E.; it originated in Central and Eastern Europe.

Yom Kippur   Day of Atonement, occurring on tenth day of Tishri. Most solemn, important fast day of the Jewish religious calendar.

Acknowledgments

Our work in Romania from 1974 to 1976 was made possible through a Fulbright-Hays grant, and through the cooperation of the Romanian government, which extended an invitation to Laurence as a Fulbright scholar.

Laurence had originally proposed to work with the Romanian Folklore Institute in Bucharest. Two colleagues there, Anca Giurchescu and Mihai Pop, were helpful in suggesting that he visit the Moldavian region to catch a glimpse of people in their "unspoiled" cultural context. It was on their recommendation that he went to Rădăuţi. He consulted with them during the course of his fieldwork; their advice and friendly support are appreciated.

The Honorable Harry Barnes, then the American ambassador to Romania, should be thanked for the personal interest he showed in this project. Both he and his wife visited us in Rădăuţi, not only to see the famous sixteenth-century painted monasteries in the region but to visit the local potter, the woodcarver, and the other good people of the town.

All the people in this book are very special to us. The townspeople, both Romanian and Jewish, were curious, courteous, and very helpful. Jacob Kamiel, the *Kultos* president, and his family officially and unofficially welcomed us into the community. The manager of the grocery store, the cook at the local restaurant, the butcher, and other shopkeepers provided

144

us with services and goods which were difficult to find in the winter months. Some evenings, when cooking at home on the one-burner camping stove became too monotonous, we went to Restaurant Nordic to hear the lively gypsy band music while sipping the strong *Tomis* Cognac. Those are now very pleasant memories. Several people in the United States and in Israel have been extremely helpful and encouraging in helping us arrange presentations and exhibits. We would especially like to thank Cornell Capa and Anna Winand of the International Center of Photography for their sensitivity and for their insights into Laurence's photography. Jesaya Weinberg of Beth Hatefutsoth Museum, Tel Aviv, generously provided us with funds and exhibit space at the museum to prepare a show of *The Last Jews of Rădăuţi* in Israel. Isaco Gaon, the exhibit designer at the same museum, should be acknowledged for his fruitful suggestions which led to the initial design of this book.

Without the generous professional help and criticisms of the following friends and colleagues, this book would have been incompletely executed: Robert Asman, a professional photographer and a competent printer, helped in printing the photographs; Janet Bloom unselfishly gave of her time and ingenuity to establish guidelines for the layout and content; Thomas Hoepker gave very useful criticisms to improve the general layout of the photographs in relation to the text. Barbara Torode put together the dummy of the book, based on the concepts suggested by Janet Bloom and Thomas Hoepker. Mark Willie, a graphic artist, created the beautiful maps; Max Rosenfeld translated the poems of Relly Blei and prepared the glossary.

Three people deserve special mention for enthusiasm that made it possible for our book to be published: Marion Stone initiated the momentum by encouraging us to find an agent for the book; Joyce Johnson and Mindy Werner, our editors at The Dial Press, had the foresight and the sensitivity to recommend the book for publication based on its merits.

The Strick Foundation and the Zuritsky family of Philadelphia have made generous financial contributions to help make the exhibit at the International Center of Photography a reality, and to finish the film *Song of Rădăuţi*, which is an indispensable part of the larger project, *The Last Jews of Rădăuţi*. Our friend, the filmmaker and editor Jonathan Greene, also contributed with his time and talents in editing the film *Song of Rădăuţi*. The Franzheim synergy Trust should be acknowledged for its generous financial contribution, which enabled the photographic exhibit to travel throughout the United States.

David and Catherine Steinmann's unfailing help and sincere interest in promoting the photographic work have provided Laurence with the incentive to continue showing this project to individuals, and thus raise the necessary funds to continue working on different phases of it.

Laurence Salzmann
Ayşe Gürsan-Salzmann

Very special thanks I reserve for my wife, Ayşe. She not only unselfishly took time off from her own research in Turkey to join me in Romania with her pet poodle, Natuf, but also contributed her insights and training as an anthropologist to help conceptualize the project. I must add that her humor and genuine interest in the people were an asset throughout the course of our stay in Romania.

Laurence Salzmann